another piece of the puzzle:
Puppy Development

Pat Hastings and Erin Ann Rouse, Editors

8/07

[signature]

DOGFOLK
ENTERPRISES

Aloha, Oregon

Published by Dogfolk Enterprises, 17195 SW Division, Aloha, Oregon 97007, (503) 642-3585.

Cover and layout design by Bridget Backus McBride, Spotted Dog Creative

Printed by Bridgetown Printing, Portland, Oregon

Visit Dogfolk Enterprises on the Internet at www.dogfolk.com
ISBN 0-9678414-2-9

Cover Photos (clockwise):
    Rhodesian Ridgebacks. Courtesy of Theresa Lyons.
    French Bulldog. Courtesy of Kathy Dannel Vitcak.
    Belgian Tervuren. Courtesy of Libbye Miller.
    Golden Retriever. Courtesy of Sheree Farber.
Back Cover Photo: Border Terrier, Courtesy of T.M. Strom.
Inside Covers: Courtesy of Peggy T. Rouse.
Previous Page: Samoyed. Courtesy of Peggy T. Rouse.

Nancy —

Never lose your "Wonderment"

of Puppies.

Pat

Parson Russell Terrier. Courtesy of Mary Strom.

table of contents

Wirehaired Pointing Griffon. Courtesy of Peggy T. Rouse.

"Outside of a dog, a book is probably man's best friend and inside a dog, it's too dark to read."

—Groucho Marx

preface

This book was inspired by the Summer 2002 issue of the Briard Club of America's magazine, *DewClaw*. It was a special issue all about puppies. I was impressed with the variety of articles about puppy rearing and training, but one article in particular really spurred me on to call Erin (while waiting in an airport) and to propose we do a book about puppy development. That article is the cornerstone and first chapter of this book. To its author, Kathy Lanam, we extend our high regard and deep appreciation, which we also extend to the Briard Club of America and the staff of the *DewClaw*. In keeping with Kathy's suggestion, a portion of the sales proceeds is being donated to Briard Health.

Our gratitude and respect also go to the other authors who contributed excellent material to this book: Diane Jacobsen, Karen TenEyck, Karen Pryor, Pat Schaap, Becca Weber, Shereen Farber, Kasmin Davis, Brenda Aloff, Lisa Branford, Kimm McDowell and Elizabeth Barrett. Most of the wisdom herein is courtesy of these fine people, and we thank them all.

Whether you're a breeder, exhibitor, performance competitor, puppy owner or prospective puppy buyer, we encourage you to read all sections of this book. What you learn may surprise you or at least make you better prepared for your next experience with puppies.

For those of you who might question our use of the pronoun "it" when referring to a single puppy, we made the choice to employ the only nongendered singular pronoun that the English language offers (at this time).

Because the information in this book is applicable to all puppies and their human mentors, we endeavored to provide plenty of photos—both instructive and entertaining. To the *many* people who sent us every wonderful photo we had the pleasure of considering, our heartfelt thanks. (We wish we could have used them all, but the book would have evolved into a coffee table album!)

For their "above and beyond" assistance, our appreciation goes to Shereen Farber, Bridget Backus McBride, Peggy Rouse, Mary and Terry Strom, and Karen Walker.

To the late Bob Hastings, we know you were with us, softly but proudly chuckling as we groped our way through this project.

Thank you, Erin, for your word sense.

Thank you, Pat, for your dog sense.

To our canine companions, past and present, we dedicate this book.

And to all of you, may you find joy, enlightenment and motivation in the reading.

"Whoever said you can't buy happiness forgot little puppies."

—Gene Hill

---

introduction: the new puppy

Babies fascinate people. It seems to make little difference whether these babies are humans, puppies, kittens, foals, ducklings or any other species–they all make us feel good. Maybe it's their vulnerability; maybe it's their innocence; maybe it is simply the wonder of new life.

Watching a foal gamboling on its long, gangly legs in a field, a batch of ducklings following their mother single file to their new swimming hole, a kitten playing with a ball of yarn or your new puppy flinging itself around the yard with absolute abandon, we find our own tenderness nourished and assuaged.

Maybe our new puppies fill caverns in our hearts through their total need to be with us or their belief that we are the most perfect of humans or their enthusiastic view of this tempestuous world. However they do it, our puppies provide a kind of sustenance that we may need in order to feel more at home in our lives.

What a profound gift our puppies offer–to make us feel better about ourselves or life in general just by curling up on our laps or looking affectionately into our eyes or happily licking, licking, licking our faces!

One definition of love is mutual regard based on trust and common interests. In the human-dog bond, the fundamental common interests are survival and companionship. Like all babies, puppies willingly trust because their survival depends on it. After their dams, we are their hope for food, shelter, care and necessary lessons. Their average life span is considerably shorter than ours, but mistakes on our part, however inadvertent, can make their brief lives confusing, frightening, lonely or overwhelming. When we consider how much their presence does for us, the most valuable gift we can give in return is to help those puppies grow into confident, healthy, self-assured, endearing members of our families–for life.

We believe the information in this book can support your good intentions and tune your perceptions of puppies and their respective potentials.

Puppies–they draw us in with those innocent eyes, those wildly wagging tails, those leaps and bounds around our clapping hands. They trust us to make their lives secure and wondrous. Dare we let them down?

chapter one

puppy development

Previous page: Rhodesian Ridgebacks. Courtesy of Pat Ottaway.
Above: Briards. Courtesy of Odile Smith.

This article was originally published in the Dewclaw (Summer 2002).
© Kathryn Lanam.

behavioral development of puppies

By Kathryn Lanam

Kathy has been a breeder since 1976, first of Standard Poodles and of Briards since 1986. She is the winner of a Maxwell Award from the DWAA and has had articles published in numerous dog magazines.

Transforming a puppy into an adult dog with the behaviors and temperament the owner needs and/or wants is a complex feat. It requires both genetic selection for a large number of physical and temperamental factors *and* appropriate social and behavioral development. The latter component rests with the breeder through the first few weeks of the puppy's life and then with the new owner. According to research by Scott and Fuller, 35% of a dog's ultimate behavioral makeup is genetic and 65% is attributed to management, training, socialization, nutrition and health care of the puppy; although the complex relationship between **nature** and **nuture** is still not well understood. Various researchers and canine behaviorists over the last 100 years have studied puppy development in wild canids, dogs in the laboratory and pets in their clinical practices. In addition, hundreds of thousands of breeders have raised puppies and observed their behavioral development throughout their lives to continually refine their puppy raising practices. Like anything else, different theories explaining canine behavior have evolved; but all agree that raising puppies correctly is mandatory if we are to maximize the potential of each puppy—stimulating its learning ability, interests and natural instincts. Old dogs can learn new tricks, but without the benefit of a good start, it really becomes a matter of playing catch up. And, sadly, millions of dogs are destroyed each year by veterinarians and humane societies as a result of inadequate training and socialization from the start.

There are several stages/periods in a puppy's life where learning and/or socialization is maximized. Behaviorists and researchers don't all agree on the exact age or influences within these stages and they may vary with different breeds. And due to several factors, puppies in a litter can vary in developmental age by two weeks even though they were all born in a relatively short period of time. Therefore a 3-week-old puppy can actually be anywhere from 2 weeks to 4 weeks in neural, physiological and physical development. This explains the variability in physical and behavioral differences seen with littermates chronologically the same age. But all behaviorists emphasize the importance of understanding and utilizing critical periods to raise the best puppies possible. According to researcher Joel Dehasse, a sensitive period (or critical stage) is a "point in the maturing process when events are susceptible to leaving long-term effects" or a period when "learning is easier and knowledge gained is stored in the long-term memory." During sensitive periods, experiences have major or even damaging effects on future behaviors of the dog. Transition from one period/stage to another is usually gradual and varies from animal to animal. The term "window of opportunity" is often used in the literature because certain experiences need to happen (or not to happen, in some cases) at a particular time, and if not, the "window" closes and the potential benefits of those experiences are missed.

Pre-Natal Period

The future behavior/temperament of a puppy begins even before birth. Many aspects of temperament are genetic and certain temperament traits are traceable through generations of a dog family. The selection process is complicated by the difficulty in ascertaining whether the temperament of a potential sire or dam is good or bad because of its genetic makeup OR the quality of its socialization and training. Certainly, sires and dams that reproduce their own less-than-desirable temperament traits should not be rebred. Most breeders believe that the dam's temperament has more influence on the puppies than the sire's—maybe not from genes, but from her role and presence with the puppies for the first 6-8 weeks. A fearful, nervous or aggressive mother (regardless of her genetic makeup) will often raise puppies with similar problems, especially without breeder intervention. Laboratory research has also shown that pregnant animals placed under stress or inject-ed with certain drugs give birth to young that are less emotionally stable and perform less well (Fox, 1978) even when raised by other mothers that weren't stressed. Exposure to parasites, poor nutrition, chemicals, disease, x-rays and drugs, especially in the first trimester, can have dangerous and lasting effects on puppies. During the third trimester, stress from extreme temperatures, inadequate nutrition and other mental and physical stresses can result in puppies with emotional and behavioral problems. Other research showed that a pregnant animal that is petted and caressed produced more docile puppies.

According to Fox (1975, 1978), this "activates the parasympathetic sys-tem, facilitating relaxation, digestion and emotional attachment." Dehasse explains this as a link to the dog's (a social species) innate need for contact. A dog's tactile capability actually develops before birth—the puppies become accus-tomed to contact in the uterus, the mother being petted, and even respond to petting themselves during late preg-nancy. Some research showed puppies from a petted mother had a greater toler-ance to handling than puppies from a mother that was not petted. Conclusions can be made that pregnant bitches in a friendly, non-stressful environment with lots of physical contact will produce puppies with a better start to life.

Figure 1-01: Beagle. Courtesy of Mary Strom and Heidiho Beagles.

Neo-Natal Period (1-14 days)

Newborn puppies are born helpless and completely dependent on their dams, responding only to the warmth, touch and smell of their dam. Newborns cannot regulate body functions such as temperature and elimina-tion. Dehasse research shows that the "position used by the puppy when licked by its mother when she is cleaning it and activating the elimination reflex will actually become a ritualized submission position used to stop agonistic behavior as a grown up dog." In short, the mother teaches the submissive position from day 1.

Neonates must have artificial sources of heat–their mother or, in her absence, heating pads, water bottles, heat lamps, etc, to maintain their body temperature. Newborns start out with a 94-96 degree F temperature and build to normal canine levels of 101-102 in the next two weeks. They are very sus-

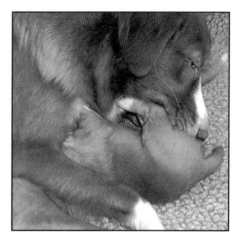

Figure 1-02: Nova Scotia Duck Tolling Retriever. Courtesy of Linda Fitzmaurice.

ceptible to excess heat and cold. Chilled puppies during this stage often develop infections, get pneumonia or have trouble digesting food, leading to "colic" or other GI stress. Many deaths of puppies during the first week can be traced to an incidence of chilling, followed by secondary infections and/or inability to digest milk. Puppies subjected to excess temperatures can also develop medical problems, including dehydration and dry eyes. Overwarm dams spend less time with their puppies and produce less milk. The

puppies sleep 90% of the time, only waking to suckle, a natural reflex in a normal puppy. The puppies crawl in a circle, moving their heads from side to side, when trying to find their mother for food and/or warmth. Their eyes and ears are closed.

There are some vocalizations at this age, especially if hungry, laid on, or in distress from digestive problems or infections. Puppy

Figure 1-03: Border Terriers. Courtesy of Peggy T. Rouse.

noise may encourage the mother to nuzzle the puppy, which helps the puppy locate the dam. EEGs at this age show that there is no difference between the puppy's brain function when awake and when asleep. Paramount at this stage is the health and happiness of the mother dog.

Too much stress at this age has a negative effect on puppies, but research (Fox; Scott and Fuller) has shown that newborns can respond to thermal, tactile and motor stimulation. Mild forms of stress create many changes in newborns including changes in electrical activity in the brain, muscle tension, and changes in oxygen levels and breathing. When tested later as adults, the stressed dogs were better able to withstand stress than their non-stressed littermates. According to Fox, they responded to stress in a "graded" fashion, while the non-stressed puppies responded in an "all or nothing" way. The stressed puppies also matured sexually earlier, were more resistant to some forms of cancer and disease and withstood exposure to cold better, were more stable, more exploratory and learned faster. Articles published by Dr. Carmen Battaglia (see www.breedingbetterdogs.com) report on research by the U.S. Military program called "Bio Sensor" or "Super Dog," also showed that "early neurological stimulation will have important and lasting effects" on puppies. He describes specific stimulation exercises for day 3 through 16 of the puppies' lives (see photos on next page). For 3-5 seconds once per day, each puppy should be:

1. Tickled between the toes with a Q-tip.
2. Held perpendicular to the ground.
3. Held head down.
4. Held on its back in the palm of your hand.
5. Lain on a cold damp towel.

These exercises should not be a substitute for the normal handling of the puppies by the breeder. More importantly, more is not better; again, too much stress is detrimental. Battaglia says "kicking the neurological system into action earlier than normal will benefit the puppy with improved cardiovascular, stronger heartbeats, stronger adrenal glands, more tolerance to stress and greater resistance to disease." Puppies were also more active, more exploratory, calmer and less distracted when working.

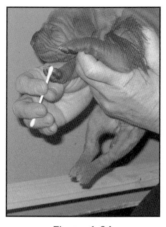

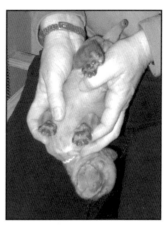

Figure 1-04:
Q-tip toe tickle.

Figure 1-05: Perpendicular
to ground.

Figure 1-06:
Head held down.

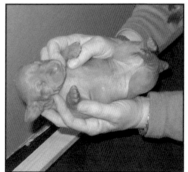
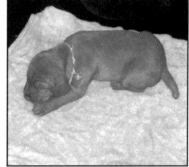

Figure 1-07: On back in
palm of hand.

Figure 1-08: On cold,
damp towel.

Vizsla photos courtesy of Karen Walker and Audrey Zatarian.

Transitional Period (14-21 days)

This period starts when the eyes are open and ends when the puppy first "startles" on hearing a noise. This week is characterized by the rapid development of motor skills, the ability to eliminate on its own, the onset of usable vision (by 18-21 days), the initial emergence of teeth, and the development of hearing—first evidenced by the startle response—although still unable to locate the source of the sound. The puppies move around a lot more, can now move backwards as well as forward and begin to walk instead of crawl, may start to lap liquids, and will begin to leave the nest to eliminate. Tail wagging begins even before developing functional sight and hearing ability, the first teeth erupt around 20 days and vocalizations become more specialized. They begin to show interest in their littermates–pawing at each other's face and chewing on each other.

Figure 1-09: Cavalier King Charles Spaniels. Courtesy of FurKids.

This is the time to begin increased individual attention by the breeder. Toys and other visual objects should be added to the box and puppies could be moved to the kitchen or other busy part of the house. Puppies should be placed on a new surface for a minute once a day (probably could coincide with cleaning the whelping box). The mother dog will begin to spend short periods of time away from the puppies this week. In this short week of life, the puppy rapidly changes from the inability to hear, see and walk or eliminate without stimulation into a puppy that can now do all of these things–enormous steps in the puppy's life.

Awareness or Identification Period (21-28 days)

Since this is the first time the puppies have use of all of their senses, they now need a stable environment and the influence of a stable dam. Sight and hearing are functioning well. A variety of noises (music, radio, bells, vacuums, etc) and sights (change in light level, moving objects and vibrations) should be part of their daily life. The exposure to sudden loud noises must happen during the 3rd week when fear has not yet developed. The startle response should be encouraged so that the pup will startle and then return to normal on its own–something it must be able to do throughout its life. Puppies must now learn that they are dogs; recognizing their mother (filial imprinting), recognizing other species–specifically humans that are part of their social relations (fraternal imprinting)–and have experiences that mean survival of the species (sexual imprinting). A poorly imprinted puppy will have problems being a "good" dog in the future. Dehasse cites several examples, including Scott and Fuller research, of imprinting "mistakes." Puppies raised in isolation from dogs at this time and then introduced to dogs at 16 weeks get attacked and rejected. Puppies without dog contact will bond with other species or inanimate objects, like a stuffed animal or even a vacuum cleaner bag. The first signs of humping (imitation of sexual behavior) begin as early as three weeks and can be stimulated by pressing on the sternum or abdomen. Breeding behavior with the wrong species may result from poor imprinting at this age. Many more examples of imprinting could be listed.

Figure 1-10: Doberman Pinschers. Courtesy of Rebecca Zaun & Marj Brooks.

Figure 1-11: Rhodesian Ridgebacks. Courtesy of Armagh Rhodesian Ridgebacks/ Jesmyster Kennels.

The puppies will begin "play-fighting" during this week, with a loose pecking order starting to form. Barking increases. They can begin to eat real food this week, but the mother should still be staying with the litter. The mother will begin growling and baring her teeth when the puppies try to nurse. The puppies will then back off or roll over on their backs in submission, and learn to keep away from the mother's teats when told. Puppies should learn one of the most important lessons in life at this time—to accept discipline.

When mothers are removed too soon from the litter, puppies do not learn this submission to adult dogs that can affect the puppy's integration (hierarchy building) with adult dogs. Wild canids and some bitches regurgitate pre-digested food to their puppies as a transition between nursing and complete weaning. Nursing can last up to 7-10 weeks, especially in smaller breeds. Extended nursing, especially in large breeds or big litters, can lead to a drain on the bitch, continued weight loss in her and extended problems returning her to working/show condition.

The less pushy puppies will also gain much slower, especially if they insist on holding out for milk and not eating food provided by the breeder. Some bitches will never wean their

Figure 1-12: Doberman Pinschers.
Courtesy of Mary Leahy.

puppies themselves and weaning must be managed by the breeder. Puppies still need a very stable environment during this time. Their humans should do a lot of handling, cuddling and pick up the puppies regularly.

Second Awareness/Identification Week (28-35 days)

During this week, play behavior becomes much more sophisticated, including growling, chasing, and "kill" games. Distance perception is much improved. Puppies should be eating real food well by now and most bitches and/or breeders will wean the litter.

Puppies need physical and mental challenges—things to move, chew on, climb on and carry, and tug toys to share with littermates. Play helps develop the strength, agility, coordination and skills to function as an adult—

Figure 1-13: Doberman Pinschers.
Courtesy of Rebecca Zaun & Marj Brooks.

Figure 1-14: Rhodesian Ridgebacks.
Courtesy of Armagh Rhodesian
Ridgebacks/Jesmyster Kennels.

whether a show dog, an agility or obedience dog, hunting dog, herding dog or coursing hound. Puppies must develop the problem-solving ability and physical and mental skills to learn and excel at these adult activities.

According to Dr. Ed Bailey, writing in *Gun Dog Magazine*, "deprived of stimulation, puppies either cannot learn or are poor learners at best." He further explains that a puppy "never experiencing and coping with frustrating situations has limited chance to develop the checks and balances of emotion" needed to problem solve and develop good temperaments. A good breeder has the "power to improve nerve conductivity in both speed and accuracy. Recovery time of the neural synapses is shortened as the chemical and electrical signals react faster and faster and the nerves can fire repeatedly quicker. The brain mass increases dramatically as nerve cell density increases." Much research backs up the conclusion that puppies raised in environments lacking challenges are more likely to develop into fearful, less successful adults.

Figure 1-15: Doberman Pinscher.
Courtesy of Dawn Danner.

Figure 1-16: Doberman Pinschers.
Courtesy of Marj Brooks.

More time should be spent individually with each puppy, observing the puppy's behavior when taken to a strange place; putting them behind a barrier and watching them; and continually adding new objects and challenges for them while alone.

Behavioral characteristics will begin to be very different when the puppy is with its littermates than when it is by itself. Separating each puppy from the litter for increasingly longer periods of time will teach the puppy independence, prevent separation anxiety problems later in life and will encourage bonding and acceptance of humans.

Socialization Period (5-16 weeks)

Dogs are not genetically "programmed" to interact socially with other species, including humans, but 12,000 years of domestication of the dog has made this possible. Living with people and adapting to their varied environments is only possible through habituation—disappearance of reactions—to certain stimuli. Many neurobiological studies have shown that the brain becomes atrophied when a dog is raised in sensorial isolation and it develops more than average in an environment of hyper-stimulation. Fox (1975) found that puppies exposed to increasingly complex stimuli—"enrichment"—would seek out complex environments; conversely, his "stimulus-poor puppies" were inhibited, fearful and looked for less complex environments. Additionally the enriched puppies were dominant in the presence of stimulus-poor dogs. The dogs lacking proper stimuli were also overexcitable, learned slower and forgot easily later in life. And a puppy raised in a deprived environment may compensate with self-destructive behaviors like coat chewing, licking, etc.

Figure 1-17: Weimaraner. Courtesy of Sue Wiley.

Figure 1-18: Rhodesian Ridgeback. Courtesy of Theresa Lyons.

Socialization does two things to habituate the puppy. It reduces the number of things in the world that a puppy might be frightened of and it continually provides the experience of first being afraid and then recovering. According to most behaviorists, bounce-back is one of the most valuable traits you can "teach" a dog. And the more often the puppy recovers, the list of things/people/experiences that the puppy is not afraid of grows faster and faster. Puppies must be exposed to a wide array of smells, textures, surfaces, sounds, vibrations, tastes and sights, including and especially a comprehensive variety of people.

The more chances a puppy has to be

Figure 1-19: Golden Retriever. Courtesy of Sheree Farber.

Figure 1-20: Weimaraners.
Courtesy of Sue Wiley.

Figure 1-21: Dalmatians.
Courtesy of Maureen Deer.

properly exposed to something new during the critical socialization periods, the less bothered it will be throughout the rest of its life when confronted by other new or frightening things. Innate fears in the canine have not been found to exist but genetic sound sensitivity is common in some breeds and some individuals. Dogs have very acute hearing and must learn to ignore the thousands of sounds that don't affect it and learn to concentrate on those that impact its life. Fears are caused from the dog's experiences in life. Everything an adult dog is expected to do or coexist with should be added to the socialization program—ie, children, swimming, exposure to livestock, dog shows, city noises, exposure to prey, gunshots, etc.

Figure 1-22: Belgian Sheepdogs.
Courtesy of Bonny Leonard.

Figure 1-23: Dalmatians.
Courtesy of Maureen Deer.

Undersocialized dogs are shy, fearful, become defensive, discriminate threats inappropriately, and may even bite out of fear. Dogs left alone for long periods of time *and* dogs that have constant human companionship are prone to separation anxiety and obsessive-compulsive disorders. If underso-cialized to dogs, the puppy may be fearful or aggressive or the other dogs may reject the puppy. When afraid, a dog reacts in a "flight or fight" man-ner, trying out different methods to deal with its fear. If unable to flee, the dog will use increasing levels of "aggression" to first scare off the feared per-son or dog and may progress to fighting or biting to defend itself. This behavioral mechanism explains why a frightened dog on a leash or restrained some other way reacts in a totally different way than if free to make better decisions about how to handle its fear, including flight–if that means has worked for the dog in the past.

Socialization requires creativity and is an ongoing process that should last the entire life of the dog and must occur during this critical period. There are many obstacles to properly socializing puppies–their owners work outside the home all day, dogs are unwelcome in most public places, own-ers avoid exposure to other dogs to reduce the risk of disease transmission, inexperienced owners/breeders don't understand dog behavior, effective puppy classes and trainers are unavailable or not deemed necessary, the own-ers stops because either the older puppies are very outgoing or they are out of control by now. The list could go on and on, but there is no substitution for intensive and ongoing socialization for *all* puppies.

This period can be further broken down as follows:

Curiosity Period (5-7 weeks)

Weaning from the dam should be complete during this period, although the mother will still play with and teach the puppies. The pup-pies will be very curious now–wanti-ng to climb, crawl, investigate and taste everything. They have very little sense of fear now and will approach and investigate anything and every-thing.

Figure 1-24: Dalmatian.
Courtesy of Maureen Deer.

Puppies have the lowest fear and the highest approach acceptance now. They are attracted and accept people sooner but peak at this time due to increased motor skills and mobility. Researchers Freedman, King and Elliot measured approach and avoidance behavior in puppies at all ages when *first* exposed to humans to make these conclusions. It's time to add scarier people and things, including children and strangers. Tunnels, boxes, steps, baby pools and other challenges should be introduced. If frightened by something at this age, the puppy will bounce back very quickly. People should call the puppy, encourage it to follow, play with, stroke, talk to, make eye contact with, and be picked up and held several times a day.

Figure 1-25: Golden Retreiver. Courtesy of Sheree Farber.

Some people call this the "gentling" process. Puppies will start rudimentary housebreaking at this time if taken outside regularly and at appropriate times, and will even start to use a doggie door.

Figure 1-26: Belgian Tervuren. Courtesy of Jill Dybus.

Of course this is the time for trips outside the house, first baths and groomings, table "stacking" and introduction to sheep/bird smells and to water (especially if expected to do water activities as an adult).

This would also be the time for ear cropping, if desired (research shows that puppies have no pain memory prior to week 7). The start to learning bite inhibition is very important during this period, both with littermates and with the human family. Clicker training and other food motivation/rewards can be intro-

Figure 1-27: Doberman Pinscher. Courtesy of Marj Brooks.

Figure 1-28: Nova Scotia Duck Tolling Retrievers. Courtesy of Linda Fitzmaurice.

Figure 1-29: German Shorthair Pointers. Courtesy of Kathy Gilliam.

duced now. Important to note is that studies show that puppies removed from the litter before the end of the 6th week will always have problems with dog-dog relationships.

Many observations can now be made about the temperament of each puppy. Breeders who spend a lot of time with their puppies, both together and individually, and provide an interesting, challenging environment for them usually "know" them well by now and are ready to temperamentally match each puppy to its new owner. Others will use some type of formal temperament testing at 6, 7 and/or 8 weeks of age to further access each puppy.

Obedience, agility, schutzhund and other working/performance enthusiasts are particularly interested in being able to predict future success in one or more of these areas. Some use the Puppy Aptitude Test, developed by the Volhards (and based on research by William Campbell– see www.volhard.com). This is a set of tests that include Social Attraction, Following, Restraint, Social Dominance and Elevation Dominance and additional obedience tests including Retrieving and Touch, Sight and Sound Sensitivity. Trainer Sheila Booth has also developed a test called "Positive Puppy Preview" which evaluates drive, persistence, focus, distractibility, food motivation, bounce-back from stress, willingness to work with a human, level of forgiveness and ego strength. Other breeders will use the services of experienced Puppy Evaluators (such as this book's co-editor, Pat Hastings) who have knowledge of both potential temperament *and* conformation. Several other variations of these tests exist but all are used to evaluate the puppy's potential for working and/or conformation showing and aid in the placement of the puppy in the right home. The results of testing will usually mirror the opinions and observations of an experienced breeder. Picking/placing the right puppy is the hope that we can "visualize" what it will be as an adult and how it will fit into each new home, lifestyle, or breeding program or will meet what's expected of a working or competitive dog.

Behavioral Refinement Period (7-9 weeks)

By 7-8 weeks puppies have fully functioning brains (as shown by EEGs) and are capable of learning anything, keeping in account their short attention spans, of course. More importantly, learning at this age is permanent. Many behaviorists agree that this is the best time for the puppy to go to its new home, unless the breeder is equipped with the time and help to treat each puppy as an individual—including crate training, housebreaking, separation from its mother and littermates for extended periods of time and extensive socialization. Many Toy breeds are also placed in new homes at 10-12 weeks—or even later—because of their smaller size, risk of injury from children and other house pets and/or some special dietary needs.

Figure 1-30: Chihuahua. Courtesy of Angela Jacobs.

Other behaviorists/breeders believe that 7 weeks is too early for placement in new homes (see "Placement Options," p. 69). Since fear in puppies is increasing rapidly during the 7th week and puppies are fearful of strangers and new situations, separation from the dam and littermates may be traumatic at this time. Scott and Fuller research also showed that the dog-on-dog (primary) socialization isn't complete at 7-8 weeks and if placed in a new home without continuing and correct exposure to dogs, the puppy will not learn to coexist in a dog world or when meeting new dogs.

Another advantage to later placement is the physical appearance of the puppy. Most American breeders believe that an 8 week old puppy is the "miniature" of what it will be as an adult, but the majority of European breeders think that the 10th week is the perfect scale model of what's to come with maturity. And there can be extreme changes in the "personality" of a puppy in one month's time too, as the additional training and socialization combines with the genetic potential to make a more predictable package. On the other side of the coin, if the breeder is not knowledgeable about correct puppy-rearing practices or does not have the time or facilities to house, train and socialize the puppies (especially a large litter of large-breed puppies), the puppies will become worse, not better, at starting on the road to becoming stable adults.

In addition, 3 or 4 more weeks of caring for the litter means many hours a day of cleaning, exercising, feeding, socializing and grooming as well as additional expenses for food, worming, vaccinations, etc. It may also mean a dilution of effort, time and money for the puppies that the breeders are keeping for themselves. Larger puppies may also be harder to transport—they cannot be carried with the new owner on the plane or need a larger crate at a higher fee for shipping in cargo.

Figure 1-31: Lab cross with Toller puppy. Courtesy of Linda Fitzmaurice.

Figure 1-32: Borzois. Courtesy of Patti Neale.

Puppies go through many, many changes during this time, bonding with their owners and learning to survive. New owners and inexperienced breeders with puppies at this age must realize how important this time is to teach puppies boundaries and the rules of their new life. Since a puppy must be taught to learn, it's imperative that the puppy learn the right things and form good habits, rather than learning bad habits that must then be modified. Emphasizing the importance of socialization and the special nutritional and health-care needs of a young puppy is crucial, as this is a period in puppies' lives when they are more likely to avoid new things and fear unfamiliar places and people. The final decision of *when* to place a puppy in the new home should probably be based on *who* is the best equipped (knowledge, time, facilities) to provide a stable learning environment for each individual puppy.

Fear Imprint/Impact Period (8-11 weeks)

Puppies have no fear until about the 5th week of life with fear increasing gradually through the 6th week and escalating toward the end of the 7th week. Between 8 and 9 weeks, overlapping the Behavioral Refinement and Environmental Awareness Period, the puppy will begin a time of much more caution. It may be fearful of loud noises, sudden movements, strangers, discipline from other dogs or humans, etc.

If frightened during this fear period, it may take weeks to return to normal. In a nonsocialized puppy, anything associated with fear at this age will always be a fearful stimulus throughout its entire life without extensive desensitization. Most agree that this is the wrong time for ear cropping, traumatic visits to the vet, shipping, harsh discipline, and maybe even transfers to new homes, especially if the new family is inexperienced with puppies. The puppies should be exposed to lots of positive experiences

Figure 1-33: Lab cross with Toller pups.
Courtesy of Linda Fitzmaurice.

at this time. Some breeders will keep a litter of puppies through this fear imprint stage to ensure that the puppy has the right experiences at this important time. This decision may also allow the breeder more time to make decisions about which puppy belongs in which home, based on behavioral development and/or conformational changes during this time. All puppies can, and many different breeds do, begin and end this stage at different ages. Unlike most other stages, the onset of this period can be very sudden. Some puppies pass through this stage very quickly and others take longer, based on a combination of genetics, socialization and the experience of the owner or breeder in handling the puppy.

Environmental Awareness Period (9-12 weeks)

Puppies still have short attention spans at this age but start to learn right behaviors for the right time, have big improvements in motor skills, pay more attention to their humans and are very busy learning about their new world. If left with their littermates at this age, they will bond with them instead of with their owner. Depending on what the owner expects from the puppy, behavior can be shaped very differently during this time. If kept almost totally separated from other dogs, the human bond becomes very strong (desirable with many performance owners) but there is a risk of the dog not acquiring good doggie social skills. If primarily kept with its littermates or other dogs in the household, the puppy will learn better doggie social skills but may have less interest in spending time with its humans. A careful compromise is probably the best answer for most puppies. Research by Konrad Lorenz and others show that attempts to change social behavior learned during this critical period are rarely successful. Puppies left with littermates through this time often have problems with excessive barking, separation anxiety and/or hyper-

Figure 1-34: Doberman Pinschers. Courtesy of Marj Brooks.

excitability. And conversely, dogs without proper dog-dog relationships (including plenty of play fighting) loose their ability to play with unfamiliar dogs and become serious about defending themselves by the age of 11-17 weeks.

Seniority Classification Period (13-16 weeks)

This time is sometimes labeled the "Age of Cutting"—cutting teeth and cutting apron strings—or the Age of Independence. The puppy begins to test dominance and leadership and "temper tantrums" are common. Puppies that have been previously very compliant will begin to have an opinion of their own and may be willing to "fight" to defend that opinion. Many puppies will bite for the first time in an attempt to do what it wants or to resist restraint. Now is the time when the various "schools" of dog training will really differ in how to handle the puppy. Traditionalists and believers of "pack behavior" will do alpha rollers and other dominance exercises to impress on the puppy its place in the "pack." Clicker trainers and others will use operant and classical conditioning to "shape" appropriate behaviors. Without contrasting the pros and cons of these different training approaches, most will agree that this is a critical period of learning for the puppy. If allowed to bite, dominate children or other pets, or resist unwanted human actions (nail cutting, lying on side to be groomed, leash training, vet exams, ear care, removing possessions or food, etc), the prospects for having a well-behaved dog in the upcoming months will be poor.

This is the time when attending Puppy Classes is essential. Even if the owner is an experienced dog trainer, the puppy needs exposure to other puppies of other breeds, sizes and temperament; needs to learn the difference between play and work; and needs to be handled, trained and disciplined by a variety of other people.

Figure 1-35: Assorted pups at class. Courtesy of Rob and Karen Perry.

An environment with lots of distractions helps build self-confidence, as does exposure to agility and other play/training equipment. An experienced instructor can help identify and prevent potential problems. The right age to start Puppy Classes is controversial. Some vets want puppies to finish their vaccination series to prevent the risk of disease (especially parvovirus), but the experienced breeder/owner knows that the potential risks from late or inadequate socialization is just as bad as that of risk of disease. A compromise between these two concerns can be made by limiting exposure to only well-vaccinated healthy dogs, being careful where the puppy is walked, etc. Be sure to observe potential Puppy Classes before enrolling to check out the cleanliness of the facilities, health requirements and training methods. Choose the training methods you (and the breeder) are comfortable with and be sure the instructors are experienced with a wide variety of breeds, the class includes well supervised puppy play and the puppies in the class are having fun as well as being guided into

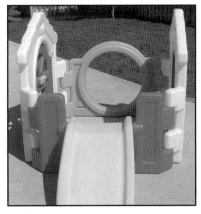

Figure 1-36: Play equipment. Courtesy of Maureen Deer.

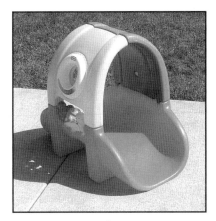

Figure 1-37: Play equipment. Courtesy of Maureen Deer.

appropriate behaviors. Most behaviorists/trainers believe that the end of this period (14-16 weeks) is also the closing of the "window" of effective socialization, so waiting until the puppy is 6 months old for class may be too late.

Flight Instinct Period (4-8 months)

This period can occur sometime between 4 and 8 months of age and can last for a few days or several weeks. The puppy will "test its wings," wander further away than ever before and its first response may be to flee. A puppy that previously came every time you called will now "turn a deaf ear" and be very difficult to catch. It's important to avoid off-leash time and to praise correct responses. Some people refer to this time as the "ha-ha-ha, you can't catch me" time. Use of a long line outside and a short leash inside (so that the puppy can never make the decision not to come) during this time will prevent accidents and actually shorten the length of time the puppy behaves in this manner.

Second Fear Impact Period (6-14 months)

Also called the Fear of New Situations Period, this period is less defined and may occur more than once as the puppy goes through growth spurts. During this period, the puppy will also be teething. Although all of the adult teeth are through the gums by 6 to 6 1/2 months of age, they don't "set" in the jawbones until 8-10 months; so even well-trained puppies will need to chew and some will become very destructive at this age if not properly supervised. A very well socialized puppy, who has been meeting and greeting the world in an outgoing happy manner, may almost overnight start to fear people and things that it wouldn't have even noticed before. This period usually corresponds to growth spurts and, unfortunately, often corresponds with a puppy's first dog shows. It's still time to socialize, socialize and socialize some more—allowing the puppy to work things out while building self-confidence. Be sure to never console a puppy who is afraid or mildly injured. Make light of the fear; introduce lots of play behavior and praise; reinforce basic obedience and attention training; and increase exercise. Dehasse characterizes this period as "the dog's anticipating harmful situations that exist only in its mind with subsequent behavioral strategies that include defense mechanisms of flight, aggression and low inhibition." Adolescence also coincides with this fear period with accompanying hormone surges, increased excitability, intensity about everything and the challenging of authority once again. Pheromones emitted by a dog can trigger dominance from other dogs, which can be very traumatic to a dog at this time. Males start to lift their leg to urinate at 5-12 months, depending on several factors including their ability to imitate another male. They develop great interest in females and can develop objectionable behaviors such as marking territory, mounting or humping, desire to roam or fighting with other dogs.

Maturity Period (1-4 years)

The maturity period signals the transition between puppyhood and adulthood. It is characterized by continual growth, both physical and mental, for up to 1 to 1 1/2years of age in smaller breeds and 2 to 3 years or more in large or giant breeds of dogs, especially intact males. As a rule, the smaller the breed, the earlier the puppy will reach sexual and structural maturity. The puppy will go from an Ugly Duckling at 1 year–leggy, thin, out of proportion, immature coat and adolescent behavior–to a Beautiful Swan, with adult coat and color, correct proportions, mature body and more stable behavior and temperament. But regular socialization must continue throughout these years. Females come into season and the male's sexual interest continues to increase. Genetically shy or submissive dogs will become even more so at this time and genetically dominant dogs can become major problems. Aggression and testing for leadership may also increase, especially in those dogs less socialized and trained in earlier months. Protectiveness increases dramatically and it's imperative that the dog is taught to discriminate fears and threats. Owners should seek help from an experienced breeder or other qualified trainer at the first sign of unusual or threatening behavior. With a genetically sound puppy and continual training and socialization through these first 3 or 4 years of life, the dog will now be "mature" in mind and body and ready to meet the owner's expectations for many years to come.

In summary, the development of a great dog is the joint responsibility of the breeder and the new owner. A mature dog's personality, physical appearance and working ability are a combination of breed characteristics, individual genetic makeup and the socialization and training it receives. Whether a puppy ever reaches its potential is in the hands of the breeder and each new owner. Understanding the social and behavioral development of a canine can help both breeders and owners prevent problems and "create" the best dog possible, whether a performance star, a beautiful show dog, a wonderful companion, a working shepherd/hunter/courser or a great parent for the next generation.

Practical Conclusions for Breeders

❖ Plan litters.

❖ Breed only healthy, good-tempered parents.

❖ Keep the dam happy and healthy before and after whelping.

❖ Provide a stimulating environment and optimum conditions for the puppies.

❖ Spend lots of time with the puppies, gentling them and helping to shape their behavior.

❖ Understand the importance of the various critical periods.

❖ Place the puppies with the right owners who can develop them to their best.

❖ Educate buyers about proper socialization, training and health-care needs.

❖ Follow up with buyers throughout the life of each puppy.

❖ Raise your own puppies to be good examples to your buyers and to the rest of the dog world.

Practical Conclusions for Puppy Buyers

❖ Choose the breed that is best for your family, home and needs. Investigate thoroughly before selecting a puppy. Avoid impulse buying or breed selection based on size, price or location.

❖ Choose a breeder who is experienced and knowledgeable of the breed, as well as knowledgeable about and committed to the effective rearing, socialization and training of puppies. The breeder should be available to each buyer throughout the puppy's life for advice and support.

❖ Be honest with the breeder about your dog experience, your lifestyle, your family and your expectations of a new puppy. Trust the breeder to choose the best puppy for your needs or use another experienced person to test and select the right puppy for you.

❖ Buy a puppy when you have the time, money and commitment to spend the next 2+ years raising, training and socializing the puppy. Attend quality puppy classes and other training classes; consult your breeder and other experts if problems arise.

❖ Follow through with your promises to the breeder in respect to health checks, breeding, etc.

❖ Understand the importance of the various critical periods and the impact you can make in each one to maximize the potential of your puppy. Learn as much as you can about the breed and the dog activities that are available or that you are interested in.

❖ Once you get a puppy, only YOU can make that puppy into the best it can be, even if simply a wonderful companion for years to come.

References

Abrantes, Roger. *Evolution of Canine Social Behavior*

Bailey, Dr. Ed. *Why Not Seven Weeks?*

Bailey, Dr. Ed. *The Forty-Ninth Day Revisited*

Bailey, Dr. Ed. *Producing Behaviorally Sound Dogs*

Battaglia, Carmen. *Early Neurological Stimulation*

Benjamin, Carol Lea. *Surviving Your Dog's Adolescence*

Booth, Sheila. *Positive Puppy Preview* (audiotape)

Campbell, William. *Behavior Problems in Dogs*

Clothier, Suzanne. *Understanding Puppy Training*

Dehasse, Joel. "Sensory, Emotional and Social Development of the Young Dog"—*The Bulletin for Veterinary Clinical Ethology* (2, 1994)

Donaldson, Jean. *Culture Clash*

Donaldson, Jean. *Mine! A Practical Guide to Resource Guarding in Dogs*

Dunbar, Ian. *Before You Get Your Puppy*

Dunbar, Ian. *After You Get Your Puppy*

Dunbar, Ian. Behavior (set of 9 booklets)—*Preventing Aggression, Socialization, Fighting,* etc.

Dunbar, Ian. *Sirius Puppy Training*

Fogle, Bruce. *The Dog's Mind*

Fox, Michael. *Understanding Your Dog*

Lindsay, Steven. *Handbook of Applied Dog Behavior and Training* (2 volumes)

Matznick, Janice. *Guide to Hand Raising Puppies*

McConnell, Patricia. *Cautious Canine*

McConnell, Patricia. *How to be Leader of the Pack*

McConnell, Patricia. *The Other End of the Leash*

O'Heare, James. *Canine Aggression Workbook*

Patterson, Gary. *"Social Behavior"* (www.siriusdogs.com)

Pfaffenberger, Clarence. *New Knowledge of Dog Behavior*

Rutherford, Clarice and David Neil. *How to Raise a Puppy You Can Live With*

Scidmore, Brenda and Patricia McConnell. *Puppy Primer*

Scott, John Paul and L. Fuller. *Genetics and the Social Behavior of the Dog*

Wood, Deborah. *Help for Your Shy Dog*

chapter two

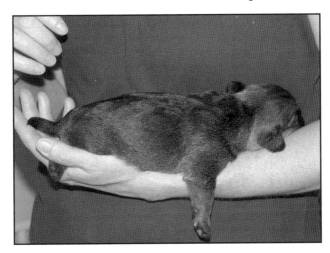

puppies and their breeders

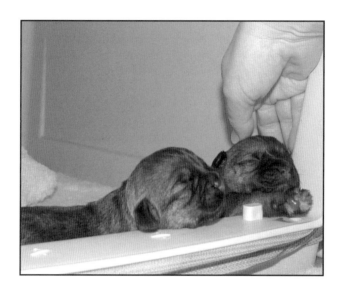

Previous page: Border Terrier. Courtesy of Peggy T. Rouse.
Above: Border Terriers. Courtesy of Peggy T. Rouse.

This article first appeared in The Ridgeback Register (April 2003).
© Diane Jacobsen

when to let go:
a veteran breeder's perspective

By Diane Jacobsen

Diane got her first Rhodesian Ridgeback in 1962 and bred her first litter in 1963. Over the years, she has produced some top winning dogs that have gone on to become top producing sires and dams. Among the notable Calico Ridge champions are Honky Tonk Hero, Mystic Talisman, California Blues, The Warlord, Solid Gold Hero, Sweet Thing, N'Tombinde, Abigail of Orangewood, Firestarter and Shot of Brandi.

The rest of the litter is doing well—nursing and sleeping—but I am really concerned over the two tiny ones. They will take special care and supplementing just because they are so small and lightweight; the bigger pups root them off the teats like piggies at the trough. I am wondering if they are strong enough to suck the milk down while they are nursing. Supplementing only goes so far, as they need that mother's milk for immunity and digestibility.

At four days, the pups are not improving. They are almost the same as their birth weight. It is now time to let them decide on their own to live or die. I back off on the supplementing to twice a day. Sometimes pups are born with a weak suckling reflex; by tube feeding, they quit trying and rely on you to feed them.

This is the part I hate. I could keep them both going by continuing to feed them, but the strongest link in the litter is only as strong as the weakest pup. The weakest will have a compromised immune system and be unable to resist the bacteria and viruses present in everyday life. After all the testing for genetic weakness, to save a weak pup could compromise the whole litter.

The smaller of the two–a female–decided that hungry was not an option and started to nurse vigorously. The other pup–a male–just gave up and quit living.

This is part of breeding and raising puppies. Are you saving a pup so that its death will not be on your conscience, or are you producing the best representative of the breed in health and body? To save a weak pup is still presenting a danger to the whole litter. That weak pup will be the first to introduce the parasites, virus, fungus, or bacterial infection to the rest.

It is the responsibility of breeders to produce the best and healthiest representatives of the breed that they are capable of producing. Can you cross your fingers and hope this pup will be a healthy representative? I can't. As much as I hate it, they must show the survival instinct–the will to fight back and the strength to make it without the constant intervention of humans.

Whelping usually goes smoothly, but one must always be on the lookout for problems. Better to have your vet regard you as neurotic and a worrywart than lose the litter. Instinct helps a lot here. If it feels wrong, go with your instincts.

After breeding for 40 years, I have never lost either a bitch or a litter. However, breed long enough and everything will happen.

a good start

By Karen TenEyck

Besides being an AKC Agility and Obedience judge, Karen has instructed classes in Obedience and Agility for 18 years and manages a large boarding kennel. She has owned and trained Shetland Sheepdogs since 1962 and has been active in her local club and the Parent club. She enjoys showing her dogs in Agility, Obedience and Conformation. Her dogs have earned several titles in performance competitions.

A dog's temperament is the product of both nature and nurture. Every puppy is born with certain genetic predispositions which cannot be changed. But environment is the other side of the equation, and this is a factor we can modify to bring out the best in puppies.

For my puppies, this process begins at birth. Every puppy is handled every day. I pick them up, put them on their backs, and gently rub their heads and backs.

After ears and eyes open, I begin playing an audiotape with all kinds of noises—including a coffee grinder, hair dryer, clapping, and various types of music—at a very low volume a few times a day. Every day, I turn the volume a little higher. This early exposure to different noises goes a long way in preventing sound sensitivity.

At 21 days, I place the whelping box in a six-foot-square pen with a plywood and linoleum floor. On the opposite side of the pen, I section off an area to fill with a litter-box material made from recycled newspaper (less likely than wood shavings to irritate sensitive eyes). One brand is called Second Nature by Purina. Even by this young age, nature is already telling them not to soil the place where they sleep–instead they will scurry over to this new area to relieve themselves. Being able to keep themselves clean at this early age makes them easier to housebreak later.

When they are about 4 weeks old, I begin adding some amenities to the pen. First are two sections of PVC pipe in "T" and "U" shapes, large enough for them to crawl through. I replace the PVC pipe with a cat tunnel when the pups are a little bigger. They explore these "tunnels" and even sleep inside them, which helps get the pups used to the idea of a crate. We also hang a tennis ball from one corner of the pen.

A week later, we add a small step stool for them to climb on or sleep under. After another week, we fasten a cookie sheet to the stool like a slide (with locking washer and screws, the end of which is cut off once the cookie sheet is attached). It's great fun to watch them try to climb up it and slide back down. We take a small bike tire wrapped with cloth tape and suspend it in the middle of the pen. One edge touches the floor, but it moves when they go through it.

As puppies graduate from the puppy pen, whether they stay here or go home with new owners, they should continue to be exposed to new experiences. These early

Figure 2-01: Parson Russell Terrier. Courtesy of Mary Strom.

Figure 2-02: Parson Russell Terrier. Courtesy of Mary Strom.

Figure 2-03: Cavalier King Charles Spaniel. Courtesy of FurKids.

experiences build the confidence and trust that are the foundation for success in conformation, performance competition, or life as a well-rounded, stable companion dog.

Golden Retriever. Courtesy of Peggy T. Rouse.

This article first appeared in the AKC Gazette (September 1999).
© Karen Pryor.

the clicker litter:
early clicker training will improve your puppies' chances of getting along in the world

By Karen Pryor

*Karen is a behavioral biologist and the author of **Don't Shoot the Dog: The New Art of Teaching and Training**.*

How soon can you begin training puppies? As soon as their eyes open, according to some breeders who are using the clicker on whole litters, even before the pups are weaned. Why would you want to do that? Well, the clicker means good things are coming. The puppy that makes that connection can then learn that its own actions sometimes *cause* those clicks that lead to treats. And the puppy that makes that discovery has a big head start on a happy future.

When to Start

Here is how it works. As soon as supplemental feeding begins, click as the pan of food is set down among the puppies. Some people click just once, and some click as each puppy nose actually reaches the food. Police officer Steve White, who breeds German Shepherd Dogs, begins clicking even earlier, every time the dam goes into the whelping box to nurse her babies (surely a very important event for the pups). You can use a mechanical clicker, a jar lid, even a pocket stapler. You need a sound that is distinct, that is the same each time, and that is different from the normal sounds in the environment. (That is why your voice is not as effective; words just do not stand out in the same way.)

After some exposure to the clicker, start taking each puppy away from the litter for a short session of its own. Click, and treat. A dab of pureed baby-food meat on the tip of the finger makes a great treat, even for the tiniest breed. Then pick something the puppy happens to do, such as lifting a front paw, and click as the paw goes up. It may take 10 or more clicks before the puppy begins lifting the paw on purpose, but then you will be amazed at how enthusiastic the puppy becomes. "Hey, look! I can make that huge person give me food. Just by doing *this*!"

Choose any simple behavior at first; it does not need to be something useful. A sit, a spin, a wave, a play bow, a back-up or a lie-down are all possibilities. You can teach all the puppies the same behavior or, if you have them identified individually, teach each one something different. Do not try to coax or lure your students into any particular behavior. You want each puppy to discover that its *own* actions make you click.

Figure 2-04: Labrador Retriever.
Courtesy of Liz Harward.

This teaches a major life lesson: "I like to find out what people want me to do." That discovery will not happen if the puppy just learns to wait to be shown what to do.

How much time does it take? Two or three clicker lessons, of no more than two to five minutes each, are enough to develop some cute little behavior. No need for a lot of drilling. Once a puppy learns what to do for a click, it will not forget. More importantly, these brief lessons can convert a puppy of 5 weeks or so from an oblivious blob into an eager, observant learner.

The Next Level

Now you can capitalize on the puppies' receptiveness to the clicker in many ways. For example, when people come up to the whelping box, do the puppies run and leap on the walls, begging for attention? Probably. So make a new rule, one that will apply to puppies, to family, and to visitors too: Only puppies that are *sitting* get petted or lifted out of the pen. It does not take long to get the whole litter sitting, and you can click them all at once. Now, when supper comes, the puppies will have to sit and be clicked before the dish goes down. Instead of repeatedly and unintentionally reinforcing jumping up, a behavior most pet owners hate, you are building a bunch of pups with better manners than that.

Come when called is another skill the whole litter can learn with clicks and treats, and a fun one for children to teach. Two or three children can take turns calling a puppy back and forth between them, clicking and treating when the puppies go to the child who called. Your buyers will get a puppy that has a head start on this important behavior.

How far can you go? Training with absolutely no corrections, just informative clicks and enjoyable treats, you can go a long way, even with a baby. When my last Border Terrier puppy arrived on an airplane, a long-distance purchase bought sight unseen, she was just 9 weeks old. I brought her home, set her down and gave her a little toy. She picked it up, carried it to me and dropped it at my feet. I thought this was surely an accident. I tossed it. She went and got it, brought it back and dropped it again. Using clicks and treats, the breeder, as a treat for me, had taught this tiny puppy a nice retrieve!

Breeders with clicker-trained litters usually give their buyers a demonstration of what the puppy has learned, a simple list of instructions or suggestions for using the clicker (several lists are available free online; search for clicker-training sites) and, of course, a clicker or two. People love taking home a puppy that already knows a trick. What a smart dog! And your early work starts them off with an attentive and cooperative pup that is ready to learn more and has a far better chance of fitting into its new world than a puppy starting from zero.

Melinda Johnson, a longtime breeder of Soft-Coated Wheaten Terriers, began clicker-training her litters several years ago. Like many breeders, Johnson will always take a dog back if it does not work out in its new home. Since she started clicker-training her litters, her return rate has dropped to zero and her file of letters from happy owners has grown enormously. These puppies still have a lot to learn, of course. But they start their new lives learning how to learn, and ready and eager to learn more.

Click!

This was originally published as part of the article "Properly Socialized" in the Potomac Valley Shetland Sheepdog Club newsletter, The Sheltie Seanachie (1987). © Pat Schaap.

the rule of 7's

By Pat Schaap

Pat, married and grandmother of 5, started obedience training with a mixed breed in 1980 and conformation showing with a Sheltie in 1985. She's been a professional trainer for 23 years, and teaching classes at all levels is her passion. She's also been breeding Shelties since 1986, with the primary goals of good structure and strong temperament.

By the time a puppy is seven weeks old, he/she should have:

❖ Been on 7 different types of surfaces—carpets, concrete, wood, vinyl, grass, dirt, gravel, wood chips, etc.

❖ Played with 7 different types of objects—big balls, small balls, soft fabric toys, fuzzy toys, squeaky toys, paper or cardboard items, metal item, sticks or hose pieces, etc.

❖ Been in 7 different locations—front yard, back yard, basement, kitchen, car, garage, laundry room, bathroom, crate, etc.

❖ Met and played with 7 new people—children, older adults, someone with a cane or walking stick, someone in a wheelchair or walker, etc.

Figure 2-05: Coton de Tulear.
Courtesy of Sandra Bearden.

Figure 2-06: Nova Scotia Duck Tolling
Retriever. Courtesy of Linda Fitzmaurice.

Figure 2-07: Dalmatian.
Courtesy of Maureen Deer.

Figure 2-08: Nova Scotia Duck Tolling
Retriever. Courtesy of Linda Fitzmaurice.

❖ Been exposed to 7 challenges–climb on a box, climb off of a box, go through a tunnel, climb steps, go down steps, climb over obstacles, play hide and seek, go in and out of a doorway, run around a fence, etc.

❖ Eaten from 7 different containers–metal, plastic, cardboard, glass, china, pie plate, frying pan, etc.

❖ Eaten in 7 different locations–crate, yard, kitchen, basement, laundry room, living room, bathroom, etc.

Figure 2-09: Weimaraner.
Courtesy of Sue Wiley.

Figure 2-10: Parson Russell Terrier.
Courtesy of Mary Strom.

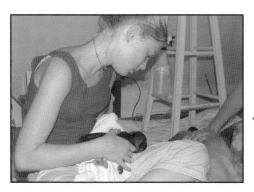

Figure 2-11: Border Terrier.
Courtesy of Peggy T. Rouse.

Figure 2-12: Coton de Tulear.
Courtesy of Sandra Bearden.

Figure 2-13: Rhodesian Ridgebacks.
Courtesy of Theresa Lyons.

Figure 2-14: Doberman Pinschers.
Courtesy of Rebecca Zaun & Marj Brooks.

Rat Terrier. Courtesy of Robin Peckham.

*This article was originally published in the Briard
column of the AKC Gazette (June 2003).
© Becca Weber.*

mental conditioning

By Becca Weber

*Becca has been actively training and competing with dogs for more than 20 years,
starting with Dobermans. In 1989, she took a Briard puppy home "for a week or
two" and became hooked on the breed. Her kennel name is Ne Orageux Briards.
She is a regular columnist for the AKC Gazette.*

All puppies need continuous mental conditioning, which must not
be mistaken for the "typical" training all dogs must have. Mental conditioning will play a large role in how dogs learn those typical training tasks.

Abused puppies/dogs are mentally conditioned to shy away from an
advancing hand, a raised foot, a sudden movement or other actions that they
may perceive as threatening. Conversely, puppies/dogs that are stroked gently about the head will move their heads toward the contact. If full attention
is withheld until the puppy/dog is sitting quietly, it is taught, or conditioned,
to sit automatically when a person approaches. These are good examples of
conditioned responses, both negative and positive. I'd like to look beyond
the conditioned response to the deeper benefits of mental conditioning—
that is, conditioning dogs to believe they can do anything asked of them.

The more mental conditioning a puppy/dog has, the greater its
potential for increased mental conditioning. It is a perfect snowball effect.
This same holds true for physical conditioning.

I condition my dogs to trust me. If I say they can do something, they
can. The only way to condition a dog to believe you is to *never* let that dog
fail. If I point a dog to a six-foot wall and order her over it without proper

training or mental conditioning, I've guaranteed her failure.

Failure to ensure the success of your puppies/dogs, even in small tasks, will condition them to lack confidence in you and in themselves. You are responsible for ensuring that their mental and physical conditioning, as well as their training, will guarantee their success. By conditioning them to believe they can succeed at whatever you ask of them, whether minor or seemingly impossible, they will not question their ability or your sanity.

Imagine being in the Best In Show ring with a dog you know is tired. It's been a long week, but here it is—the day you've been waiting for. You know the judge likes your dog. You lean down and whisper into your dog's ear: "You can do it. Just give me a little bit more." His eyes brighten and his stack hardens. He's ready to give you more.

After all, you've never let him down.

This article was originally published in the
Golden Retriever News (November-December 2003).
© Shereen D. Farber.

raising a single-puppy litter

By Shereen D. Farber, PhD, OTR, FAOTA

Dr. Farber holds degrees in occupational therapy and comparative anatomy/neurobiology and has post-doctoral training in biophysics, biomechanics and neurophysiology. She started a canine rehabilitation practice 17 years ago, in conjunction with several veterinarians, to treat and condition dogs that participate in agility, conformation, field trials and obedience. She lives with, shows and breeds Golden Retrievers.

Introduction

Raising a singleton puppy (ie, single-puppy litter) is challenging to say the least. The first two weeks of life for a singleton offers many unique concerns and can cause a breeder more worry and stress than caring for a litter of six. This article will explore strategies for raising singletons including safety, appropriate stimulation and adaptive methods of socialization and management for both the pup and the dam.

Prenatal and Perinatal Period

Once a bitch has a confirmed pregnancy, some breeders choose to do an ultrasound after day 24 in order to determine the number of puppies in the litter. Heartbeats may be seen on ultrasound by the 24th day.[1] It is not the purpose of this article to discuss the pros and cons of ultrasound, but there is an advantage to knowing in advance that a bitch is carrying a singleton or only a pair of pups.

When bitches have small litters there is a distinct possibility that the puppies may be larger than normal and prove difficult to deliver. This condition produces a possible *dystocia*—an inability of the bitch to deliver the pup without assistance. Having a labor monitoring system available and/or a vet on call seems prudent. Also, a scheduled Caesarian section may be recommended to prevent complications or death during attempts at delivery, if the vet determines that the pup or pups are unusually large. Elective C-sections require careful monitoring by the vet to detect the best time to schedule the surgery. After delivery, the vet releases the dam and pup only after they are medically stable. The breeder is instructed to check the bitch's incision daily for signs of infection and to try to prevent the pup from nursing near the incision site. Vets rarely give instructions regarding care and safety of singleton pups.

Postnatal Care for First Two Weeks

Keeping the puppy warm: Newborn pups do not have well-established thermostats making body temperature maintenance a problem. We have all seen a litter of puppies snuggled together in a pile (Figure 2-15). The puppy pile serves several purposes. Obviously, it helps puppies stay warm. Additionally, they experience the maintained pressure of puppies lying near or on them, which has a calming influence.[2] Finally, littermates lying on or near a given pup provide a wide range of sensory stimulation including smell, tactile and proprioceptive input.

How do we keep a singleton warm and simulate the experiences it would have gotten from the puppy pile? If the dam is healthy and attentive, she will usually gather her baby up and bring it near to her (Figure 2-16). Mom cannot be around every second of a new pup's life to keep it

Figure 2-15: Rhodesian Ridgebacks. Courtesy of Pat Ottaway.

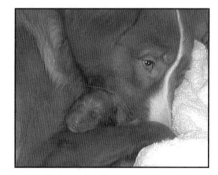

Figure 2-16: Nova Scotia Duck Tolling Retrievers. Courtesy of Linda Fitzmaurice.

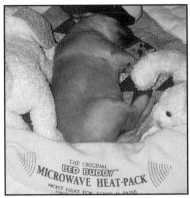

Figure 2-17: Golden Retriever.
Courtesy of Sheree Farber.

Figure 2-18: Golden Retriever.
Courtesy of Sheree Farber.

warm, nor will the singleton receive as much maintained pressure without littermates. Alternatively, I suggest using a Bed Buddy Microwave Heat Pack™ (Figure 2-17). Note that the newborn singleton has a stuffed animal of approximately the same size, pressing against its side. The Bed Buddy™ once warmed in the microwave for 2 minutes on high will stay warm for 30-40 minutes. Many breeders use socks filled with uncooked rice. While rice-filled socks are inexpensive and easy to make, the rice can burn in the microwave and the socks do not stay warm for as long a time period.

How do you simulate the sensory experience of maintained pressure that littermates provide? The breeder of a singleton should place a number of stuffed animals in the litter box and pile them around and on top of the puppy, making sure that the puppy can breathe (Figure 2-18). I recommend rubbing those stuffed animals on the mother so that they have her odor. The singleton starts to seek out its "littermates" and will continue to cuddle with them even after its temperature has stabilized (Figures 2-19 and 2-20).

Licking: Dams instinctively lick their babies in order to stimulate digestion and elimination.[3] Some dams become overly attentive and lick their singleton pups excessively, causing skin irritation and damage. The breeder must monitor for this and try to distract the dam. One breeder told me that her bitch refused to pay any attention to her singleton pup, forcing the breeder to use cotton swabs dipped in warm water to simulate the dam's licking. Another good choice for licking simulation is to use a watercolor sable paintbrush dipped in warm water. The swab or soft brush needs to be stoked across the genitalia and belly.

Bitches also lick their babies in all areas as part of grooming and survival practices. After making the puppy void, stroke the entire body with the warm, moistened cotton swabs or soft brush.

Optimum time periods: At birth, the sensory systems that are actively reporting back information are: primitive touch, orientation reflexes and smell.[3] Carmen Battaglia describes the U.S. Military "Bio Sensor" program for stimulating puppies and enhancing their performance.[4] It later became the "Super Dog" Program. The results of their research indicated that there are critical periods or windows of time when certain stimuli have maximum effects. I recommend doing the exercises developed from this research with the singleton as well as with puppies of normal size litters (see Chapter 1, p. 21-22).

Supervision of feeding: During the first two weeks, it is critical to monitor the pup's feeding by weighing it regularly and monitoring which of the dam's nipples the pup uses (Figure 2-21). Some breeders carefully rotate the puppy from one nipple to the next during the feeding. It is important to use the "stuffed animal littermates" to

Figure 2-19: Golden Retriever.
Courtesy of Sheree Farber.

Figure 2-20: Golden Retriever.
Courtesy of Sheree Farber.

Figure 2-21: Border Terrier.
Courtesy of Peggy T. Rouse.

knock the puppy off the nipple on which it is sucking. This action occurs regularly among littermates and helps makes the puppy stronger as it moves in search of another place to feed. There is something to be said for struggles making us stronger.

The dam should also be inspected twice daily for swollen or warm breast tissue possibly indicating the onset of mastitis.

Sensory Input: Tellington TTouch™

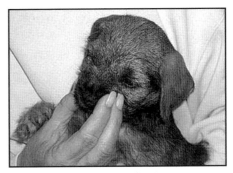

Figure 2-22: Border Terrier. Courtesy of Mary Strom.

I believe Tellington TTouch™ is useful for many different purposes.[5] I have found that it facilitates a sensory regulation, especially with Autonomic Nervous System arousal responses. After the singleton is medically stable and has survived for a week, I recommend using the gentle circular stroking method when holding and socializing with the puppy. Application of TTouch touches around the mouth helps desensitize the oral area (Figure 2-22). This will serve as the first part of bite inhibition. When a pup has littermates, it gradually learns the consequences of biting as a result of biting its littermates and hearing them cry or by being bitten by littermates and feeling the pain. A singleton needs to learn to bite softly and TTouch prevents hypersensitivity around the mouth. It also enables the pup's owner to handle its mouth and teeth.

A behavioral management program is useful for teaching the consequences of a bite by making a loud cry when the puppy bites. Of course, this is used later in development after the 4th week. Karen Pryor has advocated using clicker training with young puppies while still in the whelping box (see "The Clicker Litter" p. 51).[6]

Socialization

Battaglia states that the critical period for socialization of canines is between 4 and 16 weeks of age.[4] Joel Dehasse discusses the concept of "sensitive periods," said to be shorter time periods within the critical period. During sensitive periods, events can leave long-lasting results or a learning experience can occur more easily.[3] A few episodes of isolation may have a huge impact on a puppy during a sensitive period. Therefore, if a singleton puppy is to get along with others of its species, it is critical to introduce the puppy to other dogs before week 16 (Figure 2-23). It must learn to interact and play with dogs before that time period if it is to have normal adult interactions.[4]

Pat Hastings, AKC Judge and author, recommends in her seminars using "The Rule of 7's" (see "The Rule of 7's" p. 55-58).[7] By the time a puppy is seven weeks old, it should be exposed to at least seven different surfaces. Figure 2-06 (p.56) shows our singleton being exposed to some of the various surfaces. Hastings also endorses feeding the puppy out of seven different types of containers. The bottom line for socialization is to provide enough variety so that a puppy is not fearful of new situations, people, sounds, textures or stimuli in general.

Weaning

Many breeders of singleton litters delay weaning since the bitch seems willing to nurse for a longer time period. Generally this is not a problem unless the puppy starts to injure the dam's teats with its teeth. Continue to monitor feeding, and when the bitch is ready to wean her puppy, honor that by separating the puppy from its mother for an appropriate time period to allow her milk to dry up.

Figure 2-23: Rhodesian Ridgebacks. Courtesy of Armagh Rhodesian Ridgebacks/ Jesmyster Kennels.

Evaluation of the Singleton

Why do we breed a litter of puppies? Hopefully one answer is because we are looking to improve our breeding program. Then does that mean we automatically keep the singleton because it is the only puppy in the litter? Again, hopefully the breeder works with an objective source to evaluate the pup and ascertain if that singleton would improve the breeding program or should be placed.

I am an advocate of Pat Hastings' system of evaluating puppies.[7] It provides us with useful information regarding the structure and functional capabilities of a puppy and helps us to determine proper placements. For example, a puppy with slipped hocks, ewe neck deformity and stifles that were positioned outward would be a poor candidate for a performance home.

References

[1] Concannon, P.W. "Canine Pregnancy: Predicting Parturition and Timing Events of Gestation." *Recent Advances in Small Animal Reproduction* (International Veterinary Information Service-www.ivis.org).

[2] Farber, S.D. *Neurorehabilitation, A Multisensory Approach* (W.B. Saunders Co., 1982) pp 126-128.

[3] Dehasse, J. "Sensory, Emotional and Social Development of the Young Dog" *The Bulletin for Veterinary Clinical Ethology* (2, 1994) pp 6-29.

[4] Battaglia, C.L. "Early Neurological Stimulation Super Dog Program" www.retrieverguide.com/superdog.asp originally reprinted from *AKC Gazette* (May 1995) pp 47-50.

[5] Tellington-Jones, L. *Getting in TTouch with Your Dog: A Gentle Approach to Influencing Behavior, Health and Performance* (Trafalgar Square Publishing, 2001).

[6] Pryor, K. "The Clicker Litter. Early Clicker Training Will Improve Your Puppies' Chances of Getting Along in the World." *AKC Gazette* (September 1999).

[7] Hastings, P., Rouse, E.A. *Tricks of the Trade: From Best Intentions to Best In Show* (Dogfolk Enterprises, 2000).

Rhodesian Ridgebacks. Courtesy of Pat Ottaway.

This article was originally published in the
Petits Bassets Griffons Vendeens column of the AKC Gazette (February 2003).
© Kasmin M. Davis, DVM .

placement options

By Kasmin M. Davis, DVM

Dr. Davis received her DVM degree from Louisiana State University in 1981 and completed her internship at the University of Pennsylvania College of Veterinary Medicine in 1982. After serving three years as an officer in the U.S. Army Veterinary Corps, she went into private practice. Dr. Davis has been involved in the sport of dogs since 1980, first with Golden Retrievers and then as an exhibitor and breeder of Petits Bassets Griffons Vendeens. Currently, she is a member of the Moore County Kennel Club and the Petit Basset Griffon Vendeen Club of America.

Much has been written in dog-behavior references about the critical puppy-socialization period of 4 to 8 weeks of age. Breeders often base their placement of puppies at around 7 or 8 weeks on their understanding of this behavioral literature. Placement at this age supposedly gives the puppy ample time for socialization with littermates, yet puts it into a new home when it is most receptive to a new environment. Recently, while reflecting on the various placements I have made over the years, it became apparent that the most successful were those made with older puppies. These later placements ranged in age from 16 weeks to 12 months. Why were these dogs more successful in their new homes? Why did these puppies challenge their owners with fewer behavioral idiosyncrasies?

I believe that we as breeders, particularly those who have been involved in the sport of dogs for more than a few years, underestimate how that experience level impacts the dog's behavior later in life. When we place a puppy that is later characterized as dominant or "hyperactive" or difficult to groom, we are puzzled and can genuinely state that we have never had this problem. But is this really true? In all probability we did have this or that problem but worked through it when the puppy was young, so that it was not a major issue later in life. My show prospects are groomed frequently and have their nails trimmed often. The puppies often accompany me to the office and quickly become comfortable with crating, car rides and leash-walks in and out of buildings. They learn to interact not just with their littermates, but also with unknown and adult dogs.

What happens to this same puppy when it goes to a new pet home? In spite of my instruction to the contrary, it may or may not be taken to be groomed on a weekly basis. If the puppy rides in a car, it may well be only to go to the veterinarian. If the puppy cries or struggles during nail trims, the owners will stop, assum-

Figure 2-24: Rat Terrier. Courtesy of Lusia Kirk.

ing that they are doing something wrong. In spite of intensive socialization with other dogs early in life, a puppy may go into a home as the only dog. Will it remember the lessons learned between 4 and 8 weeks of age without constant reinforcement? Will it remember its socialization with children if it doesn't encounter another child for six months?

Many of the lessons learned by puppies during the first few months of life will be blunted without continued reinforcement. While responsible breeders ask or recommend that certain things be continued after the puppies leave our homes, the new owners—even those with the best intentions—may not be capable of following through. Our best defense against unhappy placements may well be to keep puppies destined for pet homes beyond 8 weeks of age. I have placed 16-week-old puppies that are lead trained, know a few simple commands such as *sit* and *down*, and have already had extensive experience with grooming. These lessons, carried beyond the traditional pet-placement age, seem to better prepare the puppy for the mixed messages sometimes received in novice homes.

Perhaps we as breeders would do well to reconsider the adage that 7 or 8 weeks is the "ideal" age for placement. What is "ideal" may be different for the dog going to a novice home than for a dog going to another experienced breeder.

Doberman Pinscher. Courtesy of Pat Hastings.

Tips and Tricks for Breeders

❖   Be consistent in all of your interactions with the puppies.

❖   Don't do anything for the puppies that you can teach them to do for themselves. Dams start teaching their puppies from the moment they are born; we can start teaching them once their eyes and ears are open and functioning well.

❖   Imprinting a pattern of behavior is the easiest way to teach. Reinforce their good behavior and teach them the words for what they do naturally.

❖   Encourage your puppies to do only what you would want your adult dogs to do. Teaching appropriate behavior before puppies go to their new homes significantly decreases the risk that a puppy will be returned to you because of behavior problems.

❖   The importance of early teaching on a grooming table cannot be stressed too highly. It is the most important piece of equipment you will ever own.

❖   Discourage biting as early as possible. First rule—no biting. The two best ways to discourage puppies from biting are: (1) Give a sudden, abrupt, loud, high-pitched "OUCH" or "YAWP" sound. This is what littermates would do. It must be sudden and sharp, so the puppy stops. Follow this by providing a toy. (2) Leave the room immediately. The puppy learns that if it bites, it looses your company and attention, and that is no fun at all.

❖   Don't keep littermates. Very seldom will they both reach their full potential.

❖   Let your puppies be puppies.

Puppy Packet Checklist

- ❖ Pedigree

- ❖ Contract

- ❖ Litter or individual registration

- ❖ Bill of sale

- ❖ DNA information (if any)

- ❖ Pictures of the litter

- ❖ Pictures of the sire & the dam

- ❖ Health record (including shots, worming, when next shots are due, when rabies is due, when puppy should be altered)

- ❖ Health certificates and clearances for parents

- ❖ Information about microchips and registering

- ❖ Food and feeding instructions

- ❖ A new toy and an old toy (carrying the odor of the litter)

- ❖ Puppy-teaching tips and information about training classes

- ❖ Information about joining the breed's parent club and/or a local specialty or all-breed club

- ❖ AKC information about buying a puppy/new dog

- ❖ Written material about the breed

- ❖ Information from the breed's parent club to new puppy owners

- ❖ Breed magazines and subscription information

- ❖ A copy of *Another Piece of the Puzzle: Puppy Development*

chapter three

puppies and their people

Previous page: Golden Retrievers. Courtesy of Peggy T. Rouse.
Above: Rat Terriers. Courtesy of Robbin Peckham.

what's in the hole?
know the breed before you take the pup

By Brenda Aloff

Brenda is owner and dog trainer at her center, Heaven On Arf, LLC. She authored **Positive Reinforcement: Training Dogs in the Real World** *and* **Aggression In Dogs: Management, Prevention and Behaviour Modification** *and lives with three Smooth Fox Terriers, a rescued German Shepherd Dog and a Border Collie.*

Think about a Golden Retriever or a Cocker Spaniel who encounters a deep, dark, claustrophobic hole. At the bottom is a seething, raging, red-eyed, salivating, snarling creature. Most dogs might say to themselves, "Oooooo, I bet this 'person' doesn't want me here." And after a cautious investigation, the dog will leave.

But most terriers, even at a very young age—every one, to a "man"—say: "BONSAI!!!!! I'm COMING IN!!!!!!!" Their little eyes are shining with anticipation and their tails are wagging with joy, because the possibility of a truly awesome rumble—all-out-to-the-death, hand-to-hand combat in close claustrophobic quarters—is in the offing.

It's not so much that that is what they do that's frightening, but that they are truly happiest and most alive when they are doing this.

This analogy alone should prevent anyone from wanting a go-to-ground terrier. However, there are some of us who like that living-on-the-edge feeling. And so, like idiots, we choose small, fierce, yet cheerful, monsters dressed in dog suits for our pets.

Figure 3-01: Shetland Sheepdog.
Courtesy of Cheryl Sacerich
and Sandy Schmidt.

Figure 3-02: Vizsla.
Courtesy of Candace Krout.

Figure 3-03: Nova Scotia Duck Tolling
Retriever. Courtesy of Linda Fitzmaurice.

Figure 3-04: Belgian Tervuren.
Courtesy of Sherri Eames.

Figure 3-05: Anatolian Shepherd.
Courtesy of Cheetah Conservation Fund.

Figure 3-06: Dalmatian.
Courtesy of Peggy Ann Strupp.

"It's funny, I've forgotten the names and faces of so many people who've touched my life, but I remember every detail of every dog I've known. Maybe it's because they touched my soul."

—Sue Englert

puppy nutrition

By Pat Hastings

While there is probably no perfect dog food yet developed, a diet chosen for our puppies should be "complete, balanced and wholesome." This type of nutrition is ostensibly available from many sources, but as good consumers and conscientious dog owners, we must do our homework about nutrition to find the *optimal* diet for our dog's lifestyle and age.

Accurate information may be difficult to find. The Internet is fraught with "wannabe" experts. While some veterinarians have a good knowledge of nutrition, many do not. Some breeders and owners may be passionate about the diet they provide but lack scientific rationale for the benefits. The bottom line is: If what you're feeding is working well for your puppy, do not change simply because someone tells you about another food.

Feeding tidbits from the table is fun and tempting. However, this habit can lead to the pup's dependence on table scraps instead of the complete food provided. Of course, if the complete food does not taste good, it won't benefit any puppy. A palatable diet is crucial.

Refrain from supplements. If you feel your pup needs something extra, give it some more food or switch to a food that does the job without additives.

Normal protein levels contained in most quality dog foods do not contribute to rapid growth rate or skeletal defects. The culprits in such cases are calories and calcium, not protein.

Generally, puppies should not be roly-poly fat. In fact, the trim, athletic pup is more desirable. Stay away from self-feeders or just putting a day's quantity of food in a pan. Three small feedings per day is better, eventually going down to two feedings per day.

Finally (and most importantly) read your dog, not the dog-food label. Puppies should be alert, active, inquisitive and bright-eyed. If they are not, something is amiss. Get advice from your breeder. Reputable breeders generally have done a great deal of investigating with regard to nutritional options and can offer useful recommendations. (If you don't trust your breeder's advice, you should have purchased a puppy elsewhere.)

Figure 3-07: Doberman Pinschers. Courtesy of Dawn Danner.

How do you know that what you're feeding is working? If you are feeding the correct food for your puppy, you will see:

❖ Good weight
❖ Tight feet
❖ Straight legs and pasterns (if called for in breed standard)
❖ A full coat (no bare spots) with a healthy sheen
  (not brittle or overly dry/oily)
❖ Clear, focused eyes
❖ Supple, smooth skin
❖ No inflamed or irritated membranes (eg, ears, feet)
❖ A firm stool
❖ An alert, animated attitude

Figure 3-08: Golden Retriever.
Courtesy of Sheree Farber.

Figure 3-09: Nova Scotia Duck Tolling
Retriever. Courtesy of Linda Fitzmaurice.

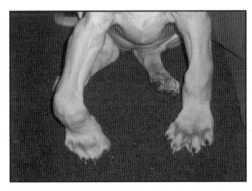

Figure 3-10: Great Dane, bad growth.
Courtesy of Linda Arndt.

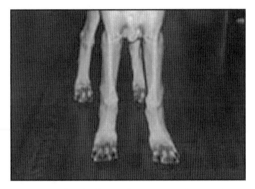

Figure 3-11: Great Dane, good growth.
Courtesy of Linda Arndt.

Figure 3-12: Doberman Pinscher. Courtesy
of Rebecca Zaun & Marj Brooks.

Figure 3-13: Briards.
Courtesy of Odile Smith.

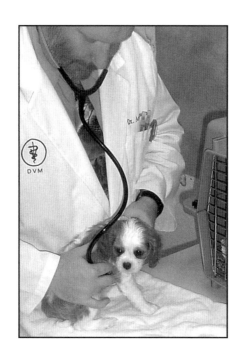

Cavalier King Charles Spaniel. Courtesy of FurKids.

vet care for puppies

By Lisa Branford, DVM

Dr. Branford, a 1985 graduate of the Washington State University College of Veterinary Medicine, has been breeding Golden Retrievers under the Brittania prefix for 20 years. Her kennel has produced numerous champions and two multiple Sporting Group winners. She has also successfully exhibited Australian Shepherds, Flat-coated Retrievers and Weimaraners.

The Well-Exam

You've done the homework—researched breeds and pedigrees, located a reputable breeder and found "the" puppy. That long-awaited day has finally come, and you're ready to take that special puppy home. Wait—there's one more step. Stop and see your veterinarian for a well-puppy check-up. Your veterinarian will evaluate general skeletal soundness and check for signs of parasites, infectious diseases and common congenital problems, such as abnormalities of the eyelids, hernias, one or more "hidden" testicles, heart murmurs and abnormalities to the nose and mouth. If your vet finds any of these conditions or other problems, it doesn't mean that the puppy needs to be returned; however, it is to your advantage to know about any potential health issues before you fall in love with the puppy—or allow your children to fall in love.

Preventative Health Care and Vaccinations

In the past few years, vaccines have become controversial, but this is unequivocal—"puppy shots" are vital. Diseases against which the most common vaccines protect include:

Canine Distemper: Outbreaks continue to occur and all puppies should be protected.

Parvovirus: Parvo is treatable but requires extensive hospitalization, and some puppies do not survive even with treatment. Again, all puppies need to be protected against this.

Infectious Canine Hepatitis/Adenovirus Type 2: Vaccinating against Adenovirus Type 2 is an excellent idea.

Bordetella: The nasal Bordetella vaccine is highly recommended for puppies attending kindergarten puppy class or spending time in other high-dog-contact environments.

Leptospirosis: If you have a large-breed dog and an active outdoor lifestyle, talk to your veterinarian about vaccinating against Lepto.

Rabies: This disease is 100% fatal and transmissible to humans. Moreover, Rabies vaccinations are required by most local ordinances. The first dose should be given some time between 3 and 6 months, and then boostered a year later. After that, a booster should be given every 3 years, unless your area requires more frequent Rabies vaccinations.

Other vaccines are available, such as those to protect against Lyme disease and Giardia. Talk to your veterinarian about the local conditions which would make these vaccines advisable.

We all realize that Western medicine doesn't have all the answers in every case and many of us know people or animals that have benefited from non-traditional treatment, including homeopathy. But as there has not been proper testing of the nosodes used in place of vaccines, they are a risky alternative for puppies at this time.

Make sure your puppies are wormed at least three times, with the final dose being followed by a negative stool check. Then follow through by taking a stool sample into the vet on an annual basis.

The parasite of greatest concern in many regions is heartworm. Check with your vet for the incidence rate in your area. Prevention is paramount with heartworm.

Common Puppy Illnesses

Vomiting and Diarrhea: First off, if your puppy is either vomiting or having diarrhea, making an appointment with your vet is **never** the wrong answer. If you have any questions or concerns, always call your vet. If diarrhea is the concern, always bring a stool sample. Using over-the-counter diarrhea remedies is not a good idea; leave the choice of treatment to your veterinarian.

Puppy Vaginitis: As the lining of the vagina in puppies is quite thin, resistance to infections is low. Affected puppies will have a sticky vaginal discharge and are predisposed to bladder infections. This condition abates with maturity; however, if you are having an issue with it, take the pup to your vet. Occasionally, a puppy will need periodic antibiotic treatment to manage the condition until the first heat cycle occurs.

Hiccups: All puppies get the hiccups. There is no cause for concern in an otherwise normal puppy.

Orthopedic Problems

These are things you need to discuss with your breeder, since each breed has its own predisposition to orthopedic problems such as Hip and/or Elbow Dysplasia, OCD, Legg-Perthes, HOD and others. As HOD is potentially life-threatening, be well aware of the signs if your breed is predisposed.

Luxating Patellas: This is a condition most commonly found in Toy breeds. It occurs when the kneecap does not stay in place and slips out of its groove. Serious cases generally require corrective surgery, but most dogs handle the surgery very well.

Panosteitis: Pano is a condition which affects large, rapid-growth dog breeds and manifests as a painful "shifting-leg lameness." Pano can start at any time but usually abates spontaneously within 6 months.

Other Considerations

Behavioral problems are a leading cause of canine euthanasia. Many of these issues are highly preventable through socialization and training. Although the threat of infectious disease is always present with puppies, exposure to new environments and situations is critical during puppyhood.

With rigorous attention to an excellent vaccination protocol and careful observation for signs of disease, a responsible puppy owner should be able to provide for the puppy's developmental needs. Although parks should be avoided, puppy classes with rigid vaccination requirements are highly recommended, as are trips to safe locations, such as relatives' homes (where the dogs are not engaged in high-dog-contact activities), grocery store parking lots (where the puppy can meet new people while in the owner's arms) and show and tell at the children's schools (with teacher permission). It's also a good idea to have a variety of people visit the puppy in its home. With proper socialization and sound, consistent training, behavioral challenges can be minimized.

There has been substantial anecdotal evidence for years that puppies kept consistently lean and in good, natural muscle condition have lower rates of orthopedic disease. Current research also indicates greater longevity and lower rates of cancer in lean dogs. If you can always feel your puppy's ribs but not see them and your puppy always has a waist when viewed from above, you are ensuring that your puppy has a greater potential for a long, healthy life.

This article was first appeared unabridged in The Rottweiler Magazine (Spring 2003). © Kimm McDowell.

preparing a puppy for the dog-show world

By Kimm McDowell

Kimm has been involved in the world of purebred-dog showing for 30 years and is a professional dog handler, obedience instructor, and breeder of Rottweilers and Cavalier King Charles Spaniels. Besides owning and campaigning several Best In Show dogs, she has successfully handled over 300 dogs to their championships.

Raising a show-quality prospect includes many things that most owners and breeders do not think about. Whether you show your own dogs or use a handler's services, I hope the following guidelines help you prepare your puppy for the lifestyle challenges it will have to face as a show dog and help your puppy develop the skills needed to grow into a well-adjusted, confident, stress-free competitor.

Feeding Practices

Do—Feed the puppies in as many places as possible, including their crates. When dogs become accustomed to eating only in their kitchen out of their own bowls, they can often be put off when fed in crates or hotel rooms or with a handler at a dog show. All of these things may occur when shown.

Don't—Feed table scraps on a daily basis (a treat once in awhile is okay). They have to learn to eat what is offered.

"Exercising" Practices

Do—Set up an exercise pen (aka "ex-pen") in your yard and make sure the puppy uses it on a regular basis, so it becomes comfortable peeing and pooping in the pen. Occasionally adding sawdust or shavings can help.

Do—Teach your puppy to relieve itself on a lead or flex lead to the command, "Go potty."

Crating Practices

Do—Crate your puppy every now and then with a treat, toy or chew bone. This helps the puppy to develop a positive association with its crate. When the puppy is tired, put it in the crate to nap.

Don't—Use the crate as punishment. (This also holds true with the use of a spray water bottle.) Both the crate and the spray bottle are important show tools!

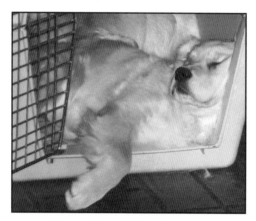

Figure 3-14: Golden Retriever.
Courtesy of Sheree Farber.

Figure 3-15: Parson Russell Terriers.
Courtesy of Mary Strom.

Baiting Practices

Teach your puppy how to catch. I use popcorn, or you can use balls of bread. Whatever you use, make it something easy to see and soft, so it won't hurt if you hit the pup between the eyes.

Do—Teach the command "Catch" (or "Cookies"). After the puppies learn the "Catch" game, use different types of treats including liver, chicken and cheese so the puppies are trained to bait for anything.

Don't—Allow puppies to chase down the missed treats on the ground. This will teach them to watch the floor at a show. They are only allowed to pick it up if you tell them it is okay. Most of the time, pick it up and give to them.

Figure 3-16: Shiba Inu.
Courtesy of Pat Hastings.

Showing Practices

Do—Teach the puppy to stand on a table or a box. Praise it for standing still for a few seconds, and then gradually increase the amount of time.

Do—Get as many people as possible to ask your puppy to "show teeth."

Do—Get the puppy comfortable with strangers running their hands over every part of its body.

Don't—Push the puppy past its point of tolerance. Never get angry with your puppy when working on these practices. These must be positive experiences. Anger or impatience could turn these exercises into confrontations.

Do—Teach your puppy how to walk nicely on a lead. Encourage the puppy to walk slightly ahead of you.

Don't—Let your puppy pull or drag you while on a lead.

Grooming Practices

Do—Teach your puppy to enjoy bath time. Start bathing your puppies while they are young. They don't have to like it but they do have to tolerate it. Try to make it as positive an experience as possible.

Do—Teach your puppy to have its nails trimmed/ground weekly. This is essential to the well-groomed show dog. I personally prefer grinding the nails. Teach the puppy to stand on the table to have its nails cut or ground without an argument.

SOCIALIZE, SOCIALIZE, SOCIALIZE.
See you at the shows!

Belgian Sheepdog. Courtesy of Lauren Paul.

picking your agility puppy

By Elizabeth Barrett

Elizabeth lives in Georgia, where she and her husband, James, breed and exhibit Doberman Pinschers in conformation, obedience and agility under the kennel name of ADAMAS. They have bred and/or handled three Doberman Pinscher Club of America Top 20 Agility Finalists.

Though many potential puppy buyers believe that puppy temperament testing is the major component in selecting a performance prospect, my breeding and training experiences have led me to different conclusions. First and foremost to me is structure.

In agility, it does not matter how wonderful a dog's drive and willingness to please is, if it is structurally unsound. Agility is a high-impact sport, putting a great deal of stress on the body through jumping, sprinting, ducking into tunnels, sharp turning and weaving. Poor conformation opens the dog up to multiple types of wear, tear and injuries. High drives, trainability and willingness to please are all moot traits if an agility dog's career is cut short by its body's inability to withstand the physical rigors of the sport.

Evaluating Structure

When selecting an agility prospect, I look for the same sound structure and function as when searching for a conformation prospect. The only major difference would be that, in an agility prospect, there is no need to consider the head, unless it is so disproportionately large as to make it a liability to the stability of the cervical (neck) vertebrae.

As a breeder, my initial evaluation comes when my newborn puppies are still drying. I look at the shoulder layback, length of upper arm and croup proportions. Assuming you are not the breeder, and with the breeder's permission, the next step in evaluation comes at around 4 weeks, when the puppies are walking competently. It is surprising that at such a young age, well put-together puppies begin to stand out in the litter. I look for the puppies that can handle themselves well—that is, ones that walk steadily and

Figure 3-17: Shiba Inu. Courtesy of Pat Hastings.

that stop "four square." By "four square," I am referring to a puppy that stands well *into* its front assembly and makes full use of its rear angles. A puppy that "rocks back," "A-frames" or "posts" off of its front end, and/or a puppy that stands "sickle-hocked" or with the rear legs slightly tucked up and not stretched out and perpendicular to the ground, is not standing "four square."

As I continue to watch the litter develop over the following weeks, I observe how the puppies use themselves. As they age and gain greater self-awareness, more puppies in the litter may emerge that can handle themselves and also stand "four square." Further observation usually reveals that these same puppies tend to move in a comfortable trot rather than the bunny lope of their littermates. In my experience, the puppies that can handle themselves well at an early age (4-9 weeks) will grow into adults that are very in-tuned with their bodies, know where their feet are (important for the dog walk, teeter and weave poles) and are proficient jumpers. Starting around 6 weeks, the puppies can be hand-stacked for evaluation. Stacking in front of a mirror can help you get a better viewpoint. However, puppies at this age rarely stand still long enough for a proper evaluation, so it's beneficial to have someone stack the puppy while another takes pictures for more deliberate scrutiny later. Once again, I am looking for the same physical structure I would want in a conformation prospect:

Overall balance: As I look at the puppy as a whole I want to see overall balance–height to overall length and depth of body to length of leg. I do not want to see any areas of the body that are extreme and out of proportion to the rest of the body. While most think of extremes as too much of something (ie, excessive rear angulation or excessive forechest), the reverse can also apply–such as a back or neck that is too short, or the front or rear assembly that is too straight. All of these are extremes and should be recognized for what they are–deviations from the standard of the ideal for most breeds, limitations to the achievement of optimal physical performance, and areas for potential weakness, breakdown and injury.

Front assembly: Much has been written over the years about the importance of correct front assembly. This is no less true in agility where the front is responsible not only for the initial lift in jumping, but more importantly, for bearing the entire impact and weight of the dog upon landing.

Quoting from *Jumping From A to Z* by M. Christine Zink, DVM, PhD, and Julie Daniels: "When the shoulder blade is more vertical [often referred to as upright or straight shoulders], three things happen. First, there is a reduction in the range over which the scapula-humoral joint [the joint between the shoulder blade and the upper arm] can extend. This reduces the amount by which the dog can stretch the front legs forward [reach] and results in a shortened step length. Second, upright shoulders reduce the ability of the front legs to absorb the weight of the dog's body as the feet hit the ground, both when gaiting and when jumping. This increases wear and tear on the shoulder and elbow joints, which absorb the majority of the impact during movement. Third, dogs with upright shoulders have less area available for the muscles that extend between the shoulder blade and the upper arm. This can reduce the strength of the forelimbs and thus affect performance."

In regard to short upper arms, Zink and Daniels say, "The shorter the upper arm, the closer to vertical the upper arm will be when the dog is standing. The effect is similar to that of an upright shoulder, a reduction in the ability to reach forward, reduced muscle mass between the scapula and the upper arm, and hence a reduction in the length of stride and an increase in concussion. The effects of an upright shoulder and shortened upper arm are additive. Active performance dogs with both

Figure 3-18: Dachshund.
Courtesy of Mary Mackin.

problems are much more prone to shoulder injuries and have greater chance of developing arthritis of the shoulder and/or elbow."

Strong, straight, parallel front legs give the dog stable support, while tight cat feet and firm, barely sloping pasterns assist in sharp turns and shock impact.

Rear assembly: Like the front assembly, the rear should be well proportioned and conform to the breed standard.

The rear assembly provides propulsion for running as well as for jumping. The current fad in conformation is for more and more rear angulation. While greater rear angulation does mean greater prospective propulsion, instability increases proportionately. Conversely, insufficient angulation offers greater stabilization but poor propulsion and limits extension (drive).

Back: The back should neither be too long or too short. Too long of a back will be insufficiently supported and susceptible to undue stress. This is particularly true in the area of the unsupported lumbar (loin) vertebrae and in the area where those vertebrae meet the thoracic (back) vertebrae, as well as just forward of thoracic seven where most dogs carry their center of gravity. Too short of a back will not have the flexion needed for optimal jumping and turning.

Evaluating Temperament

The idea of testing puppies for temperament and aptitude for prospective working careers has been around for decades. Standardized tests, such as the one administered at 49 days, are readily found in many books.

Steve Frick, a member of the 2001 AKC Gold World Team, prefers to start assessing a litter as soon as the breeder will allow it—from birth if possible, but at least no later than 4 weeks of age—when looking for agility prospects. He also likes to be able to meet the sire and dam of the litter, as much of the litter's temperament will be extracted from them.

Steve admits that due to a lack of understanding of the subject, early on in his career he did not pay much attention to the structure of a prospect. "Now that I have Comet [his World Team Border Collie partner], I know what physical attributes I want in my future dogs, such as a well laid back shoulder and interchangeable front and rear . . . . It doesn't matter how wonderful the dog's temperament is, if it can't jump."

Like Steve, I also have never been a fan of using a standardized puppy test, but rather prefer ongoing observation for such aspects of the test as sound sensitivity, dominance, following, social attraction and retrieving. I have found that observation of my litters over the weeks of their development and early socialization are more beneficial than a single administered test.

Additionally, I have found puppies that would have scored extremely poor in standardized puppy tests can grow into exceptional dogs providing they have an owner committed to working through the puppy's weak areas. When Piper, one of my current agility dogs, was perhaps 4 to 5 months old, a fellow exhibitor remarked what incredible toy drive she had. I explained that in reality the bitch did not have any natural toy drive, but rather I had clicker-trained the drive into her.

I have two puppies that can handle themselves well and are very comparable structurally—square, very good layback of shoulder, long well-returned upper arms, strong backs, moderately angled rears, strong pasterns and tight feet. One is an outstanding agility/obedience prospect, while I would never consider placing the other in a home wanting a performance dog. The first puppy is outgoing, confident, sociable, comfortable with restraint, always comes when called and follows happily. He retrieves toys and eagerly runs toward strange, loud noises, assuming it must be something he can play with or eat. He boldly plays on new obstacles placed in the yard. The second puppy is more reserved, independent, dominant, self-rewarding, will chase a ball and then run away with it, struggles fiercely and vocally when restrained, tries to bite when having his nails done. This puppy's temperament is not suitable in any performance arena.

One must weigh carefully both physical structure and disposition when looking for an agility puppy. Some disposition issues can be resolved if the owner is willing to commit the time and effort to work with the puppy. However, once set by genetic code, structural weaknesses cannot be corrected, and any resultant damage may be irreparable.

"Your Future Agility Prospect"
    By Elizabeth Barrett
    Published in *Doberman Digest* (dobedigestm@aol.com):

    Part 1: "The Role of the Breeder" (April 2003)
    Part 2: "Picking Out Your Agility Puppy" (June 2003)
    Part 3: "Optimizing Your Puppy's Potential" (August 2003)
    Part 4: "Laying the Groundwork to Formal Training (October 2003)

"Dogs are not our whole life, but they make our lives whole."
—Roger Caras

preparing a puppy for the real world

By Pat Hastings and Erin Ann Rouse

Our world can be a crazy place, filled with myriad sights, sounds, smells, adventures and hazards. It is replete with critters and people, speeding cars and lumbering trucks, potholes and fences. It is a grassy park one minute and crowded city streets the next. Even in the sanctuary of one's own home there are phones ringing, something cooking, dishwashers sloshing—well, there's always something.

Into this ruckus we bring puppies, and like all innocents, they must be taught how to face the challenges of what may come their way. First their mothers, then their breeders and finally their human families have the pleasure and responsibility to teach them what's safe and what's treacherous, what's expected and what's unacceptable. This task requires a commitment of time, love, patience, consistency and dispassion. The rewards are puppies that grow up to be as comfortable with themselves and the world around them as it is possible for each individual puppy to be.

Besides ensuring that our puppies are well nourished, relieved from the elements, and protected against disease and parasites, the best we can do is to help our pups develop the ability to learn and the ability to think for themselves.

Teaching Puppies to Learn

Puppies may be born with curiosity but not with a quest for knowledge; we must teach them to learn. And the more they learn, the more they want to learn.

Determine the rules of the house (no biting, no messing in the house) and be consistent in enforcing them. Teach puppies words for what they are doing–be it sitting, tail wagging, walking, holding their paw up. The more words they learn, the larger their internalized vocabulary becomes. Teach them good behaviors by rewarding them with affection, praise and a treat. Discourage unwanted behaviors by withholding your attention or redirecting them toward an acceptable behavior. For example, if the puppy starts chewing on your shoe, hand the pup a toy and praise it for turning its attention that way.

Set the puppy up to succeed. If the puppy isn't ready to learn a complicated task, wait until the time is right in the puppy's development for it to succeed (see "Mental Conditioning" p.59).

Teach, teach, teach, and they will learn, learn, learn.

Figure 3-19: Briard.
Courtesy of Sandy Brown.

Figure 3-20: Doberman Pinscher.
Courtesy of Dawn Danner.

Teaching Puppies to Think

Like all children, puppies need to work through challenges; they need to figure things out for themselves.

If we see that they're going to bump into a tree and we prevent the collision, they lose the opportunity to figure out that trees won't step aside and they need to look where they're going. If we see that they're going to step one foot off the edge of a grooming table and prevent it, they lose the opportunity to figure out that tables have edges.

Figure 3-21: Briard.
Courtesy of Dorte Bhutho.

Figure 3-22: Parson Russell Terrier.
Courtesy of Mary Strom.

Another significant example is when our puppies meet adult dogs. Well-socialized adult dogs are the only ones who can teach our puppies doggie manners. If our puppies are obtrusive or obnoxious with adult dogs, the adults will usually give the puppies a sharp, succinct reprimand. In this way, puppies learn doggie manners. If we intervene, thinking that our puppies are being threatened, they lose an opportunity to learn doggie lessons about polite social interaction.

When we teach our puppies nothing, they grow up to be seemingly brainless dogs. Over-protective actions on our part can diminish a puppy's budding confidence and encourage uncertainty and anxiety instead.

Puppies are better than that. They are bright and responsive if we nurture their intelligence. They can work through challenges, and we must give them those opportunities.

Figure 3-23: Rhodesian Ridgebacks.
Courtesy of Theresa Lyons.

Figure 3-24: Briards.
Courtesy of Odile Smith.

Encouraging these abilities helps our puppies adapt in a complex world that demands their basic understanding of a crazy place beyond their own front door. The stronger their abilities, the greater their enthusiasm for new challenges and the more their self-confidence shows in their eyes, the set of their ears, the sureness of their posture and the swipes of their tails.

Our puppies are wholly dependent on us to help make their futures joyous and fulfilling. We can either help them flourish or founder, and if we choose the former, we may well find ourselves flourishing right along with them. After all, a dog's passion for living can be profoundly contagious. And lighting the mind and spirit of youngsters (no matter what the species) enriches both the guides and their charges. It is perhaps one of the best definitions of love.

Tips and Tricks for Puppy Owners

- ❖ Be fair in your interactions with the puppy.

- ❖ Set and maintain a regular routine with the puppy (eg, mealtimes, potty times, walks, etc). Routine provides puppies (and dogs) a sense of security. However, puppies also need stimulus to help them build confidence in new situations.

- ❖ Provide a crate for your puppy as a safe haven. It is a den, not a punishment.

- ❖ Feed 3 small meals daily; leave food down for only 20 to 30 minutes.

- ❖ If your new puppy isn't drinking much water, add a couple of drops of lemon juice to its water.

- ❖ Have a set area outside for eliminating. Encourage the puppy to eliminate right before a play session or taking the pup for a walk (the play session or walk becomes a reward).

- ❖ If the puppy wears a collar, it is much easier to leash-train.

- ❖ Don't let your puppy make mistakes—prevent them from happening. This is much more than just house breaking. For example, coat all exposed electrical cords with dish soap so the puppy looks for more palatable items to play with, like puppy toys.

- ❖ Don't ever let your puppy do anything that you would not want your adult to do.

- ❖ Don't do anything for your pup that you can teach it to do for itself.

- ❖ Don't train – teach.

- ❖ When teaching or training, use a small treat to reinforce every command every time.

❖ Discourage biting as early as possible. First rule—no biting. The two best ways to discourage puppies from biting are: (1) Give a sudden, abrupt, loud, high-pitched "OUCH" or "YAWP" sound. This is what littermates would do. It must be sudden and sharp, so the puppy stops. Follow this by providing a toy. (2) Leave the room immediately. The puppy learns that if it bites, it looses your company and attention, and that is no fun at all.

❖ Let your puppies be puppies.

Wirehaired Pointing Griffon. Courtesy of Peggy T. Rouse.

Border Terrier and Vizsla. Courtesy of Erin Rouse and Loren Jones.

resources

Article-Specific References

"Behavioral Development of Puppies." See Pages 41-42
"Raising a Single-Puppy Litter." See Page 67

General References

American Kennel Club (AKC), www.akc.org
Association of Pet Dog Trainers (APDT), www.apdt.com
Dr. Carmen L. Battaglia, www.breedingbetterdogs.com
Elizabeth Barrett, www.AdamasDobermans.com
Companion Animal Recovery (CAR), 800-252-7894, www.akccar.org
DogRead, www.dogread.com
DNA Operations and Education Services, 919-816-3508,
  dna@akc.org
Orthopedic Foundation for Animals (OFA), www.ofa.com
Karen Pryor, www.clickertraining.com
Tellington TTouch, www.ttouch.com

Books

Born To Win, Patricia Craige, www.doralpub.com
Canine Reproduction – A Breeders Guide, Dr Phyllis Holst,
  www.alpinepub.com

Don't Shoot the Dog, Karen Pryor, www.dogwise.com

How To Speak Dog, Stanley Coren, www.dogwise.com

Jumping From A to Z , M. Christine Zink, DVM, PhD, and Julie Daniels, www.caninesports.com

Successful Dog Breeding, Chris Walkowicz and Bonnie Wilcox, DVM, www.prenhall.com

Tricks of the Trade: From Best Intentions to Best In Show, Revised Edition, Pat Hastings with Erin Ann Rouse, www.dogfolk.com

Publications

AKC Gazette, An American Kennel Club Publication, 800-533-7323

DewClaw (request for back issues), Christi Leigh, Editor, cdleigh@nmia.com

Doberman Digest (request for back issues), dobedigestm@aol.com

The Family Dog, An American Kennel Club Publication, 800-490-5675

Ridgeback Register, www.theridgebackregister.com

The Whole Dog Journal, A monthly guide to natural dog care and training, www.whole-dog-journal.com

Micro Chip Information

Avid, www.avidid.com

Home Again, www.homeagainid.com

On-Line Shopping

Amazon Books, www.amazon.com

DogWise Books, www.dogwise.com

Canismajor, www.canismajor.com

PetEdge (formerly New England Serum Company), www.PetEdge.com

Videos

"Puppy Kindergarten," Corally Brumaster, www.clickertraining.com

"Puppy Puzzle: The Hastings Approach to Evaluating the Structural Quality of Puppies," Bob and Pat Hastings, www.dogfolk.com

Samoyed. Courtesy of Peggy T. Rouse.

Doberman Pinscher. Courtesy of Dawn Danner.

It takes more than luck to win in the ring.

You have to do your homework to win, and one of the most informative resources has been Pat Hastings' book, **TRICKS OF THE TRADE: FROM BEST INTENTIONS TO BEST IN SHOW.**

Dogfolk Enterprises is proud to announce the FULLY REVISED EDITION of this best-selling book, coming out in 2004. Based on Hastings' Tricks of the Trade seminar that captivated dog fanciers for 15 years, the revised edition takes up where the first edition left off, with a greater store of information and illuminating visuals.

This book has something for everyone involved in the sport of purebred dogs, but you may have to uncross your fingers to turn the pages.

DOGFOLK
ENTERPRISES

Lead off with dogfolk.com